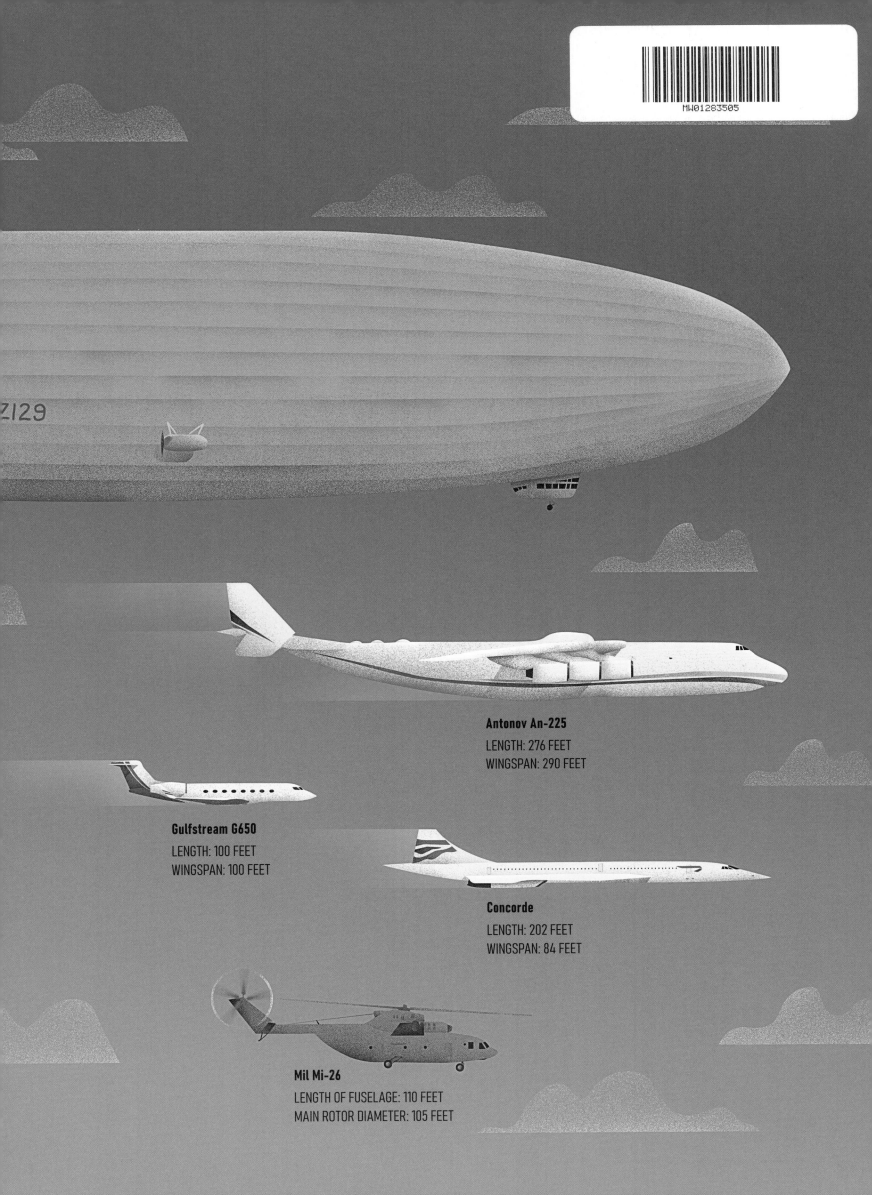

Z129

Antonov An-225
LENGTH: 276 FEET
WINGSPAN: 290 FEET

Gulfstream G650
LENGTH: 100 FEET
WINGSPAN: 100 FEET

Concorde
LENGTH: 202 FEET
WINGSPAN: 84 FEET

Mil Mi-26
LENGTH OF FUSELAGE: 110 FEET
MAIN ROTOR DIAMETER: 105 FEET

https://kids.britannica.com/kids/article/airplane/352719
This site gives information on different types of aircraft and their history, as well as explaining how airplanes work. Comprising simple explanations and pictures that will help readers understand even complex topics, it is a rich source of information for children interested in science and technology.

www.123homeschool4me.com/how-airplanes-fly-lesson-for-kids/
This site contains lessons on aviation, including various experiments and activities for children to try at home. Although targeted at children of primary-school age and their parents, it is ideal for teachers who wish to include practical activities in their lessons.

https://outschool.com/online-classes/aviation
This link will take you to online interactive courses for children and youngsters on various topics of aviation. The courses cover the history of aviation, how aircraft work, drones, and many other matters.

www.aviastar.org/helicopters.html
This site is for readers interested in helicopters.

www.onverticality.com
This blog for those with their head in the clouds appeals to their interest in tall buildings, mountain tops, and, of course, aviation.

UP, UP, AND AWAY

THE HISTORY OF AVIATION

WRITTEN & ILLUSTRATED BY

TOMÁŠ SMOT SVOBODA

 albatros

HELLO FRIENDS!

You've opened this book just in time. My grandchildren Molly and Simon are waiting here in my study. I'm going to the kitchen to get the goodies Grandma Elizabeth has prepared for us. While I'm gone, why not explore the room so you know what we're going to talk about today?

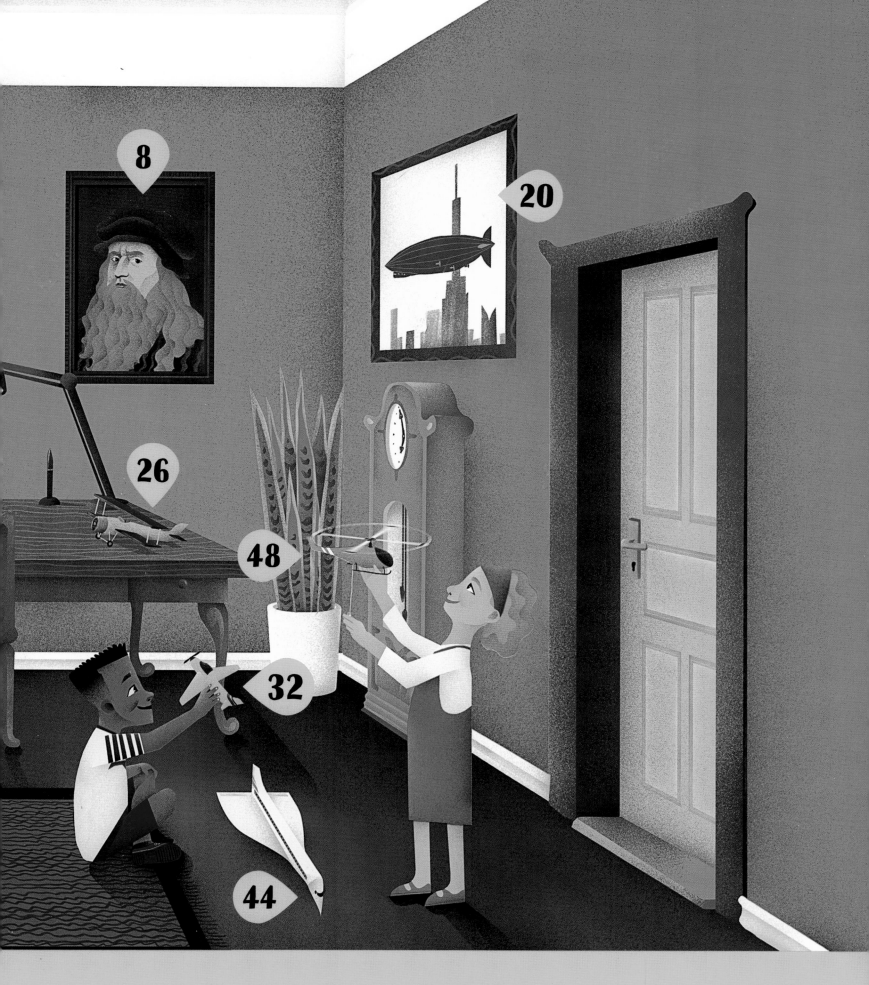

AN AGE-OLD LONGING TO FLY

People have always dreamed of flying. Early humans watched birds in the sky and wondered how they did it. What must such freedom feel like? But before we get to today's modern airplanes, we must pass through a great deal of trial and error, and many adventures and sacrifices.

IT STARTED IN GREECE

In Ancient Greece, the gods were believed to rule from atop Mount Olympus. In Greek mythology, a fictional architect and inventor named Daedalus lived with his son Icarus on the island of Crete after fleeing from Athens.

LUCKY BIRDS, FLYING ABOUT WHILE WE CAN ONLY WALK!

OW! WHAT A HEADACHE

DON'T FEAR THE TAKEOFF

On Crete, Daedalus supposedly built a mysterious labyrinth for King Minos, where the fearsome Minotaur – half-man, half-bull – was kept. Only the Athenian hero and future king Theseus would be able to defeat him.

INSPIRED BY BIRDS' WINGS

Daedalus longed to return to Athens, but King Minos refused to let him leave, fearing he would reveal the secrets of the Labyrinth. Daedalus knew the only way to escape the island was by flying. He made two pairs of wings from bird feathers and wax, attaching one set to his own arms and the other to Icarus's. Before taking off, Daedalus warned his son to fly behind him.

I'LL FLY HIGHER THAN PEGASUS!

But Icarus didn't listen to his father. Overcome with the thrill of flight, he soared too high. The sun melted the wax on his wings, causing them to fall apart. Icarus plunged into the sea. Daedalus, heartbroken, buried his son on an island that came to be known as Icaria, and the place where Icarus fell was called the Icarian Sea.

ICARUS! NO-O-O!

BIRDS' WINGS

A bird's wings are indeed made for flying, but so is the rest of its body. Birds have powerful flight muscles and strong hind limbs. Their skeletons are lightweight yet very strong, making up only about 4% of their body weight, compared to up to 30% in mammals. Their hollow wing bones are filled with air and connected to their respiratory system. The feathers are also very light and help keep the bird's body temperature high.

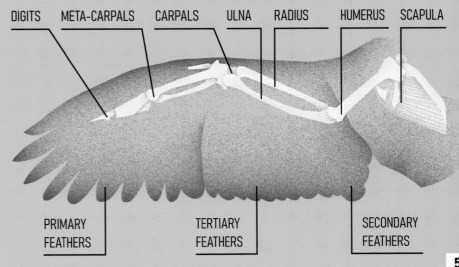

DIGITS META-CARPALS CARPALS ULNA RADIUS HUMERUS SCAPULA

PRIMARY FEATHERS TERTIARY FEATHERS SECONDARY FEATHERS

FROM GREECE TO ASIA

The story of Icarus is a myth that uses flight as a symbol of freedom. Moving east to China 2,500 years ago, the philosopher Mozi and a legendary man named Lu Ban were both linked to kite-making, though kites existed much earlier. These early kites – made from wood, bamboo, and cloth – were often shaped like birds. The secrets of kite-making stayed in China for many years before spreading to other parts of the world.

MOZI

LU BAN

USEFUL KITES

On windy days, people often fly kites for fun. Today, kites are mostly enjoyed as a pastime, but long ago, they served important military purposes. In China, kites were used to measure distances and communicate over difficult terrain, much like ships use flags at sea. Kites were also used to gauge wind strength and direction. According to the Chinese legend, Mozi even created a kite large enough to carry a person. While this folklore story didn't really happen, what a cool story it is!

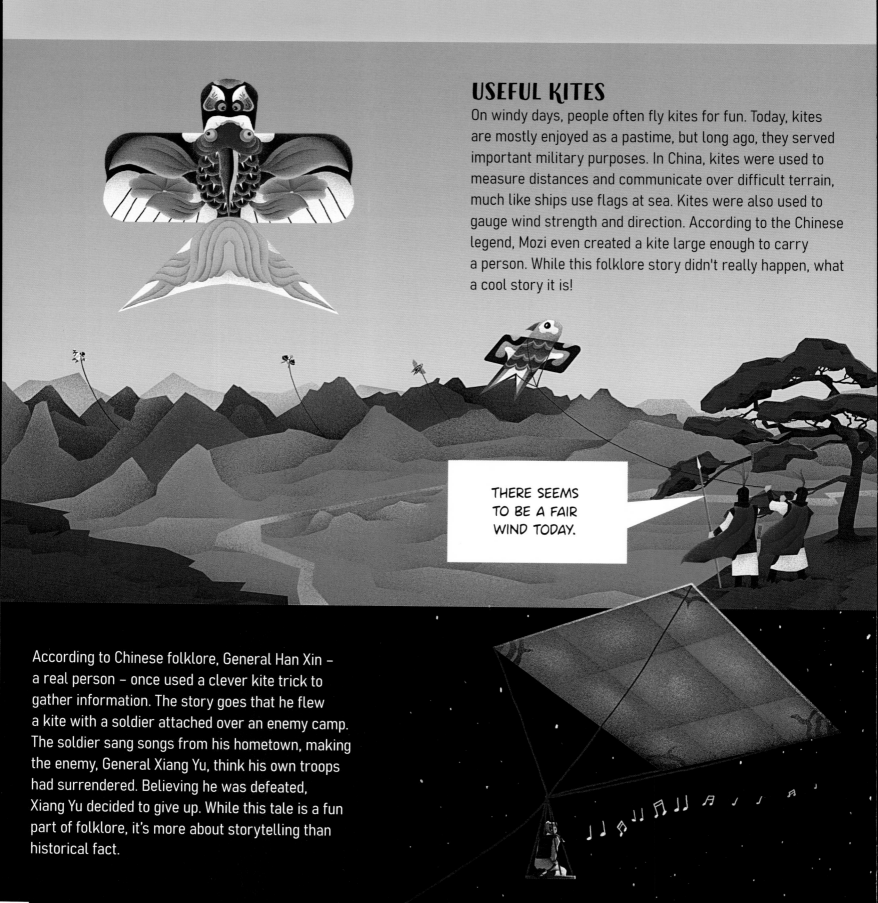

THERE SEEMS TO BE A FAIR WIND TODAY.

According to Chinese folklore, General Han Xin – a real person – once used a clever kite trick to gather information. The story goes that he flew a kite with a soldier attached over an enemy camp. The soldier sang songs from his hometown, making the enemy, General Xiang Yu, think his own troops had surrendered. Believing he was defeated, Xiang Yu decided to give up. While this tale is a fun part of folklore, it's more about storytelling than historical fact.

LEGENDARY MEN ON KITES

In 1282, the famous Venetian explorer Marco Polo wrote about seeing massive kites in China. Later legends claimed people flew on them, but this is unlikely. However, kites were used to lift objects, guide ships, measure distances, and test winds.

KITE ADRENALINE

On seaside holidays, people sometimes attach themselves to a parachute and get pulled behind a motorboat. This is a bit like what happened in Ancient China, where people used kites in a similar way. Today, **parasailing** is a fun sport, and so is **kitesurfing**, where a kite pulls you across the water while you ride a kiteboard.

2. PIONEERS OF FLIGHT WHO DIDN'T FLY

THE ROCKY ROAD TO THE AIRPLANE

The journey from paper kites to real flying machines took a long time. It took many years for people to understand how birds fly. In the meantime, inventors created all sorts of strange and amazing flying machines, one after another. None of them, however, could achieve controlled flight.

SMART AND BRAVE

Countless clever minds worked on flight. One of the earliest was Abbas Ibn Firnas – a scientist, inventor, philosopher, alchemist, and poet. In the year 852 CE, he made aviation history by jumping from a mosque tower in Córdoba, Spain, using a cloth sail attached to a wooden frame. Although he broke a few bones, he is credited with making one of the first parachute jumps. In 875 CE, he achieved even more: in front of hundreds of witnesses, he successfully flew a glider from the La Arruzafa hills near Córdoba.

A SILK SAIL OVER A WOODEN FRAME DECORATED WITH DIFFERENT BIRD FEATHERS

AM I MISSING SOMETHING?

GLIDERS

If Firnas invented the glider 1,000 years ago, why didn't we start flying properly until the 19th century? Before the internet, news and discoveries didn't spread quickly, and many inventors and their ideas were simply forgotten. For instance, an English monk named Eilmer, who lived around the year 1010 CE, jumped from the tower of Malmesbury Abbey with a contraption similar to Firnas's. He flew about 650 feet before crashing and breaking both legs.

HOW DO BIRDS DO IT?

In the old days, people closely observed birds to understand how they could fly. They learned that birds use their wings by flapping and gliding to create enough lift and speed to overcome gravity, which pulls them down, and air resistance, which slows them down.

DYNAMIC LIFT

SPEED

RESISTANCE

GRAVITY

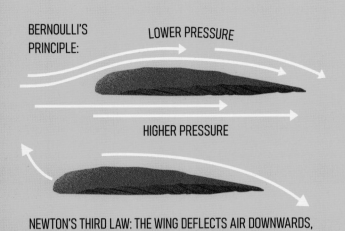

BERNOULLI'S PRINCIPLE:

LOWER PRESSURE

HIGHER PRESSURE

NEWTON'S THIRD LAW: THE WING DEFLECTS AIR DOWNWARDS, THEREBY CREATING A FORCE THAT PULLS IT UPWARDS.

AIR AND ITS POWER

Birds glide by using their wings and the airflow around them. The air pressure is higher below the wing than above it, and this difference creates lift. This is known as Bernoulli's principle.

Newton's Third Law of Motion, named after Sir Isaac Newton, a famous scientist, is a rule of nature that says for every action, there is an equal and opposite reaction. This means that when a bird pushes air down with its wings, the air pushes the bird up with the same force. This helps the bird fly.

AIR AS A TRAMPOLINE

Each flap of a bird's wings creates something called "dynamic lift." This means the bird pushes against the air, which helps it stay in the air and rise higher. When the bird flaps, it might drop a little, but it also goes faster, thereby bouncing off the air and fly higher.

SPEED AND GLIDING

While gliding, a bird must keep moving forward to stay in the air. This forward movement causes it to descend slightly against the airflow, but it doesn't fall towards the ground. When the bird encounters rising air currents, like those near a hillside, this descent helps it rise relative to the ground.

UPDRAFT

TO GLIDE WITHOUT FLAPPING THEIR WINGS, BIRDS USE "UPDRAFT" – A CURRENT OF RISING AIR THAT LIFTS THE BIRD UP, HELPING IT SOAR HIGHER.

FEATHERED MUSE

The bird is to aviation what the muse is to the artist – an inspiration! A perfect example of this is the genius artist Leonardo da Vinci. His ideas for flying machines, based on bird flight, were far ahead of his time.

RENAISSANCE MAN

Leonardo da Vinci painted the *Mona Lisa*, the most famous painting of all time. Besides being a brilliant artist, Leonardo was also an inventor, architect, sculptor, naturalist, musician, designer, and engineer. He lived in Italy during the 15th and 16th centuries, a period known as the Renaissance.

ON THE FLIGHT OF BIRDS

From a young age, da Vinci was fascinated by flying. He made detailed studies of how birds and bats fly, examining their wings closely. His notebook, called the *Codex on the Flight of Birds*, includes an impressive 1,700 drawings spread across 1,600 pages.

IDEAS ON FLYING

He also designed an ornithopter, a type of flying machine that's heavier than air and powered by people. His notes included ideas for the wings, how they would flap, and how the ornithopter would land. Since no complete drawing of the machine has been found, we don't know exactly what it looked like. However, there is some evidence that da Vinci built and tested the ornithopter in 1504. It was said that his assistant flew it for several miles from the hills of Fiesole, but this is almost certainly untrue.

PRINCIPLE OF HELICOPTER FLIGHT

In addition to designing winged flying machines, Leonardo also imagined the idea of helicopter flight. He envisioned a machine with an "aerial screw," which would be powered by four people running in circles.

OVERHEAVY MACHINE

Staying on a merry-go-round for too long can make you dizzy. That might be why Leonardo never built his aerial screw. It would have been difficult to control and far too heavy to lift four people into the air. Still, Leonardo's idea was very important for the future of flying machines.

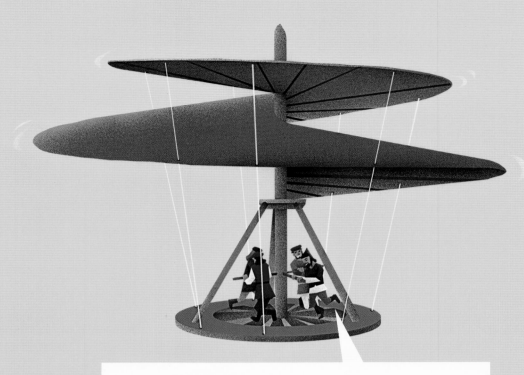

I SHOULDN'T HAVE HAD SECONDS AT LUNCH.

EVERYONE WILL BE FLYING IN A YEAR.

I WOULDN'T WISH TO UPSET YOU, SIGNOR LEONARDO, BUT I'D SAY IT'LL BE MORE LIKE SEVERAL CENTURIES.

RENAISSANCE PARACHUTE

Among the celebrated inventor's notes and sketches, there is a design for a parachute shaped like a pyramid. It had four equilateral triangles with sides over 20 feet long. In 2008, Swiss amateur parachutist Olivier Vietti-Teppa became the first person to build and successfully use one, jumping from a height of over 2,000 feet.

BIRDS AREN'T EVERYTHING!

A Portuguese-Brazilian priest named Bartolomeu de Gusmao, who lived in the 17th and 18th centuries, designed an airship called the Passarola. He was inspired by the shape of a bird's body for the hull of the airship. The ship would have a large sail to catch the wind and keep it in the air. If there was no wind, bellows and tubes would blow air into the sail. The airship would be powered by a system of magnets inside two hollow metal balls.

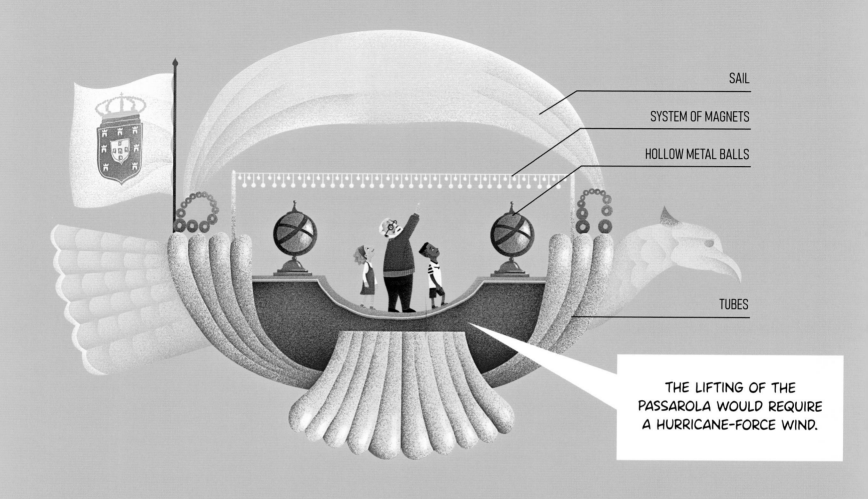

SAIL

SYSTEM OF MAGNETS

HOLLOW METAL BALLS

TUBES

THE LIFTING OF THE PASSAROLA WOULD REQUIRE A HURRICANE-FORCE WIND.

SO WHEN DO WE GET TO THE PLANE?

The Passarola didn't look much like a bird. Instead, there were three more modern machines that use elements found in today's aircraft. The first is Dr. William Orville Ayres's unusual pedal-powered machine, notable for its three types of power and many propellers.

DANGEROUS MACHINE

It does look odd – and pretty dangerous too. If it had been built, using this pedal-powered machine would have been super risky. A wrong move could have caused injury from the fast-spinning propellers, not to mention the loud noise from the motor. This shows that flying machines are not only created by inventors; even ordinary doctors can have inventive ideas.

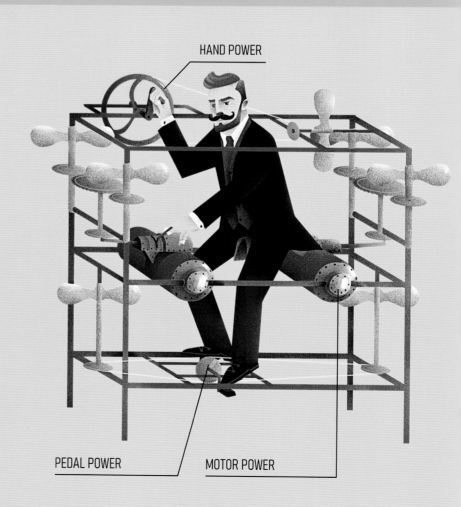

HAND POWER

PEDAL POWER

MOTOR POWER

AERIAL STEAMER

The second machine had wings. Named the Aerial Steamer, it was designed by English engineer Thomas Moy. This aircraft had two propellers and three wheels, just like some modern planes. The propeller blades were over six feet in diameter, and the wingspan was more than 13 feet. The Aerial Steamer didn't have a pilot and was powered by a steam engine created by Moy and Richard Edmunds. An attempt to fly it was made in June 1875, but the engine was too weak to get it off the ground.

THREE-WHEELED
UNDERCARRIAGE

THE MACHINE WEIGHED OVER 200 POUNDS. MOY CALCULATED
THAT TAKE-OFF WOULD BE ACHIEVED AT 35 MILES PER HOUR.
THE STEAM ENGINE MANAGED ONLY ABOUT 12 MILES PER
HOUR, HOWEVER.

A PILOT AT LAST!

The last of our three aircraft would have carried up to 12 passengers. Named the Aerial Steam Carriage, it was designed in 1842 by William Samuel Henson and John Stringfellow. It had a wingspan of 148 feet and was powered by a steam engine. Although the designers had success with smaller models, they couldn't get their larger versions to fly. The Aerial Steam Carriage was never built to full size, and its steam engine was too weak to achieve flight. Also, the wing design wouldn't have provided enough lift.

EXHAUST OUTLET FOR
EXPULSION OF STEAM

WE'RE FLYING! HOORAY!

Balloons were the first machines that were lighter than air. They floated because they were filled with hot air or gas. At the end of the 18th century, when the first balloons were flown, the so-called "aeronauts" who took to the skies became famous and were celebrated as heroes for their bird's-eye views from above.

HEROES IN BALLOONS?

In those days, no one knew what would happen to a rising balloon. People worried that at great heights there might be no air to breathe or fly in. So the first public balloon flights had no crew. In June of 1783, the Montgolfier brothers introduced their balloon, which was filled with hot air. That August, French physicist Jacques Charles launched a hydrogen-filled balloon. The world's first aeronauts weren't humans – they were a duck, a sheep, and a rooster that flew over the Palace of Versailles that September. Their flight in the Montgolfier brothers' balloon was watched by King Louis XVI, the entire French court, and 130,000 amazed onlookers.

BLESSED COINCIDENCE

The Montgolfier brothers, Joseph-Michel and Jacques-Étienne, came from a family of 16 children. But only the two of them were interested in flying. After reading about a gas called hydrogen in Joseph Priestley's book *On Different Kinds of Air*, they started experimenting. Since they worked with paper, they first tried to put hydrogen in paper bags, but the gas always escaped. They also tried using steam, but it condensed on the bags. In 1782, they got a lucky break. After walking in the rain, Joseph-Michel's wife was drying her clothes by the fireplace. The hot air from the fire lifted her skirt slightly, and Joseph-Michel had an idea. Just a week later, in the yard of their paper mill, the brothers launched their first small hot-air balloon. Their invention was so successful that they were knighted for it. Today, hot-air balloons are still known as "montgolfiers" in their honor.

JOSEPH-MICHEL MONTGOLFIER

JACQUES ÉTIENNE MONTGOLFIER

FLIGHT ON A ROPE

The first recorded human flight took place on October 15, 1783 in a balloon made by the Montgolfier brothers. The person who made this historic flight was Jean-François Pilâtre de Rozier, a French physicist and aviation pioneer. The balloon was tethered to the ground with a rope, and it reached a height of 85 feet.

NOW WITHOUT THE ROPE

Rozier is best known, though, for making the first manned free hot-air balloon flight. On November 21, 1783, he and François d'Arlandes took off from the garden of the Château de la Muette in Paris. The wind carried them across the Seine River, and they landed safely on the outskirts of Paris after a 25-minute journey. This was a major milestone in aviation history.

Sadly, Rozier and Pierre Romain also became the first fatalities of an air crash, when their balloon exploded during a later attempt to fly across the English Channel.

MEN IN THE CLOUDS? THEY'LL NEVER BELIEVE THIS AT HOME.

WE'VE DONE IT, DEAR ROZIER! WE'RE FLYING!

F_b BUOYANCY

F_G GRAVITY

THE SECRET OF THE BALLOON

Balloons fly because they are filled with hot air or a gas like helium or hydrogen, which is lighter than the air around them. This makes the balloon rise, much like how a beach ball floats on water. Gravity pulls the balloon down because of its weight and the weight of its basket and passengers. For the balloon to rise, the lift from the lighter gas must be stronger than gravity. This idea is explained by Archimedes' principle – named after the Ancient Greek mathematician and inventor Archimedes – which says that an object in a fluid (like air or water) will float if it pushes aside enough of that fluid to balance its own weight.

CONQUEST OF THE ENGLISH CHANNEL

On January 7, 1785, French balloonist Jean-Pierre Blanchard and American physician John Jeffries became the first people to successfully cross the English Channel by balloon. They took off from England and reached France, but not without a challenge. As the balloon started losing altitude toward the end of the flight, they had to shed as much weight as possible, eventually even discarding most of their clothing. For his daring achievement, Blanchard was awarded a lifetime pension by the king and became famous across Europe for his public flights. He even toured the USA, showcasing his skillsto many people, including President George Washington.

SWIFT AS THE WIND

Balloon races are not always about speed. One of the most famous and oldest competitions is the Gordon Bennett Cup, where balloons compete to see which can fly the farthest. The current record, set in 2005, is held by Bob Berben and Benoît Siméons from Belgium, who flew an incredible 3,400 miles in 65 hours! There are many other balloon competitions too, like ones for accuracy of landing, chasing another balloon, or flying the least distance while trying to stay in the air for a set amount of time.

BALLOONS IN WARTIME

Up until World War II, balloons were mostly used by the military. Tethered above battlefields, they served as observation points, letting crews drop messages or shout instructions through a megaphone. Balloons were also used in the early days of aerial bombing.

LET'S SEE, WHAT'S THE ENEMY HAVING FOR BREAKFAST?

USES OF BALLOONS

Balloons weren't just for the army. The post office used them to deliver letters and packages. Nowadays, meteorologists use small balloons with special instruments called "radiosondes" to gather information on things like temperature and air pressure up to 18 miles high. Modern helium-filled balloons even help astronauts explore the edges of outer space. Balloons are also popular for sightseeing flights and fun races that people enjoy watching.

A BALLOON 560 FEET IN DIAMETER AND 400 FEET HIGH CARRYING AN INSTRUMENT (WEIGHING HALF A TON) FOR MEASURING COSMIC RADIATION WAY UP IN THE STRATOSPHERE, ON THE EDGE OF SPACE.

WHERE'S ITS RUDDER?

A balloon can't be steered like a car or plane. It goes wherever the wind takes it. However, the pilot can control the balloon's altitude by making it rise or fall. Since wind direction and speed can change at different heights, the pilot might use these changes to guide the balloon to a certain area.

FIRE, THE GOOD SERVANT

Burners in the basket of a hot-air balloon are used to heat the air inside, which makes the balloon rise. When the burner is turned off, the air cools down, and the balloon begins to fall. There's also a vent at the top of the balloon to let out the hot air, helping to control its altitude.

THE ADVANTAGE OF GAS

A gas balloon doesn't have a burner. Instead, it uses sandbags as ballast to control its altitude. By dropping sand from the sandbags, the balloon becomes lighter and rises. To make the balloon fall, the pilot releases some of the gas through a vent, similar to the one in a hot-air balloon. A gas balloon can stay in the air for several days if it doesn't release too much gas.

WIND DIRECTION

TO FLY OVER THAT CASTLE, WE NEED TO RISE.

HOT AIR OR GAS?

Hot-air balloons are usually bigger than gas balloons because hot air needs a larger space to create enough lift. In contrast, gases like hydrogen and helium are lighter than air and can lift a much smaller balloon while still providing the same buoyancy.

EARLY BIRDS

Balloons are often seen in the early morning because the sun heats the air and creates warm updrafts, known as thermals. These updrafts help lift the balloon into the sky. By midday, when the sun is strongest, the heat can cause the balloon to overinflate and potentially burst. Therefore, balloons are usually flown in the morning, evening, or during cooler seasons. They don't fly in the rain or snow due to the risk of damage and reduced visibility.

BALLOON FILLED WITH HOT AIR

BALLOON FILLED WITH GAS

COLOR IS NICER

Balloons are often colorful to make them look more cheerful and eye-catching. Their bright colors and designs help them stand out from afar, almost like a moving billboard. Balloons don't have to be round – they can come in all sorts of fun and unusual shapes.

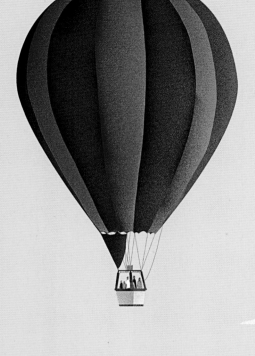

3 ... 2 ... 1 ... LIFT-OFF!

A hot-air balloon takes off in a few steps. First, the balloon is inflated with cold air while it's still on the ground. Once there is enough cold air inside, the pilot turns on the burner to heat the air. This makes the balloon start to rise. The pilot and crew climb aboard only when the balloon is almost ready to take off. Before the balloon can lift off, the ropes that keep it tied to the ground must be untied.

ENVELOPE

The envelope is the big, colorful part of the hot-air balloon that holds the hot air. It's made from strong fabrics like polyester or polyamide, which are coated to keep the air from escaping. This helps the balloon stay filled with hot air and rise into the sky. The design also makes sure that the weight of the basket is supported by the vertical supports.

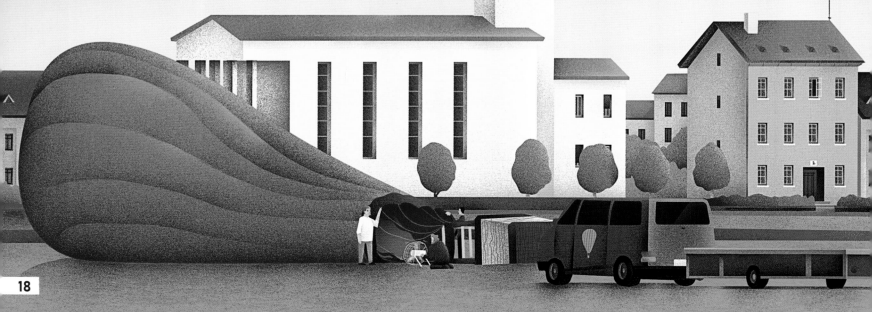

BLAST VALVE

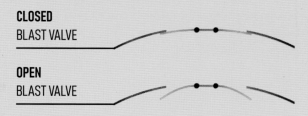

CLOSED
BLAST VALVE

OPEN
BLAST VALVE

Blast valve – located at the top of the balloon. It's used during flight to help control the balloon's altitude by letting out hot air from the bag. This allows the pilot to make the balloon go up or down as needed.

Burner – the balloon's burner usually has one or more units. It heats the air inside the balloon to make it rise. The main burner does most of the heating. There's also a silent burner used to avoid scaring animals when flying over farms. The pilot burner helps light the main burner.

ROPE FOR BLAST
VALVE CONTROL

CABLES HOLDING
THE BASKET AND
ENVELOPE TOGETHER

BURNER

BASKET

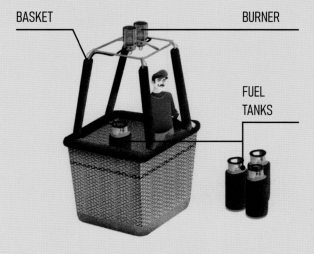

BASKET

BURNER

FUEL
TANKS

The basket – carries the crew and all the equipment needed for the flight, including the fuel tanks. The sides are made of woven wicker, and the floor is made of waterproof plywood. The edges are padded to make the ride more comfortable for passengers.

Fuel tanks – these hold the liquefied gas needed to run the burner. They are padded for protection and stored directly in the basket.

4. CELESTIAL GIANTS

GIANTS OVERHEAD

The biggest machine the skies have ever seen is the airship. Like a balloon, an airship is a lighter-than-air craft. It first appeared in the late 19th century and was most popular in the early 20th century. These giants – some over 650 feet long – could be steered and had engines that allowed them to reach speeds of over 60 mph. They could fly against the wind and across entire oceans. However, with the development of airplanes, which were faster, safer, and cheaper, airships became less common. Even so, the occasional airship can still be seen floating overhead.

GRAF ZEPPELIN

D-LZ127

FLYING CIGARS

Airships are called "ships" because they were so big and moved through the sky like ships move across the sea. The names of their parts were taken from the names used for sea ships. In 1783, a French inventor named Jean-Baptiste Meusnier first conceived of their football shape, which helps them fly smoothly.

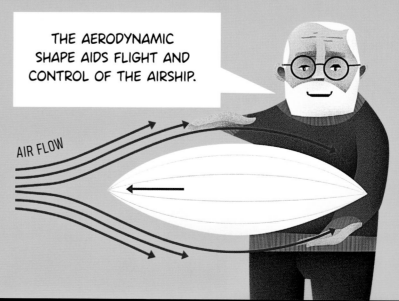

THE AERODYNAMIC SHAPE AIDS FLIGHT AND CONTROL OF THE AIRSHIP.

AIR FLOW

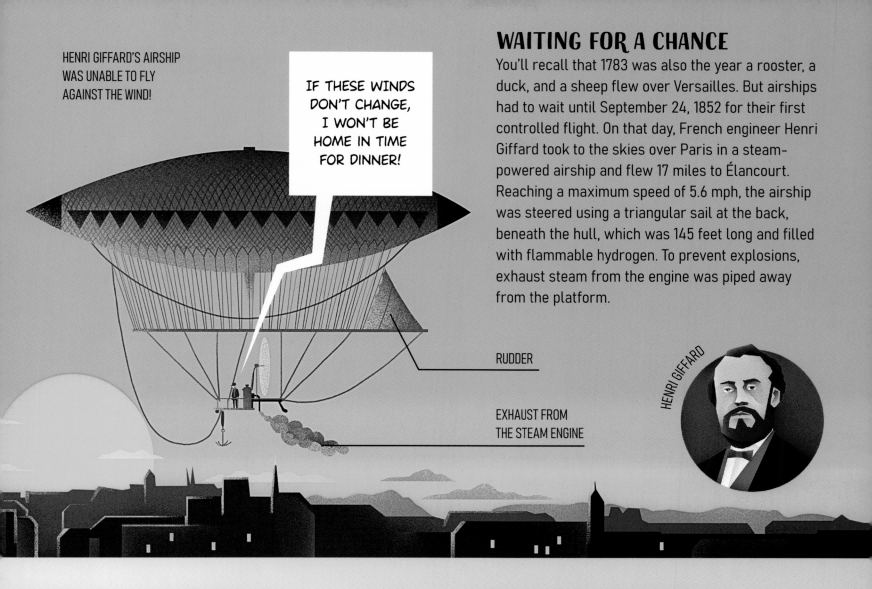

HENRI GIFFARD'S AIRSHIP WAS UNABLE TO FLY AGAINST THE WIND!

IF THESE WINDS DON'T CHANGE, I WON'T BE HOME IN TIME FOR DINNER!

RUDDER

EXHAUST FROM THE STEAM ENGINE

HENRI GIFFARD

WAITING FOR A CHANCE

You'll recall that 1783 was also the year a rooster, a duck, and a sheep flew over Versailles. But airships had to wait until September 24, 1852 for their first controlled flight. On that day, French engineer Henri Giffard took to the skies over Paris in a steam-powered airship and flew 17 miles to Élancourt. Reaching a maximum speed of 5.6 mph, the airship was steered using a triangular sail at the back, beneath the hull, which was 145 feet long and filled with flammable hydrogen. To prevent explosions, exhaust steam from the engine was piped away from the platform.

CHEAP BUT COMBUSTIBLE

Hydrogen was chosen because it was easy to get and didn't cost much, even though it can catch fire. It wasn't until the 1960s that most airships started using helium, which doesn't catch fire. Giffard also faced a challenge with his steam engine – it was not powerful enough to help the airship fly against the wind for the return trip to Paris.

THAT CURSED HEADWIND!

Giffard didn't wait for the wind to change, although it wouldn't have helped. The first airship to make it back to its starting point was a French airship named *La France*, on August 9, 1884. With its electrical engine and large propellers, this 164-foot-long airship could fly at 12 miles per hour and handle a light headwind. Charles Renard and Arthur Krebs built and flew *La France*.

THANKS TO ITS POWERFUL ELECTRICAL ENGINE, *LA FRANCE* RETURNED TO ITS STARTING POINT 5 TIMES IN 7 FLIGHTS.

A LOOK INSIDE THE ENVELOPE

An airship's envelope can have different designs. In one type, known as a **non-rigid airship**, the envelope is filled mostly with gas, and it keeps its shape because of the pressure of the gas inside pushing against the air outside. As the gas can expand or shrink with changes in altitude, there are special compartments inside the envelope called ballonets that hold air. The pilot can inflate or deflate them during flight to balance the pressure and help keep the airship steady. Many early airships were designed this way.

The next type of airship is called a **semi-rigid airship**. Inside the envelope, there's a long beam called a keel that runs from the front to the back. This keel helps keep the shape of the airship and holds up the cabin, engines, and other parts. Along with the gas and a ballonet, the keel makes sure the airship stays steady in the air. This kind of airship made its first successful flight on November 13, 1902, and some airships today are built like this.

The third type is called a **rigid airship**. It has a strong frame made of materials like aluminum that supports the whole airship. The gas inside is kept in separate sections, or cells, that are built into the frame. This type was designed by David Schwarz, a Croatian inventor. Unfortunately, he passed away before seeing it fly. Rigid airships are famous for being used in Zeppelin aircraft.

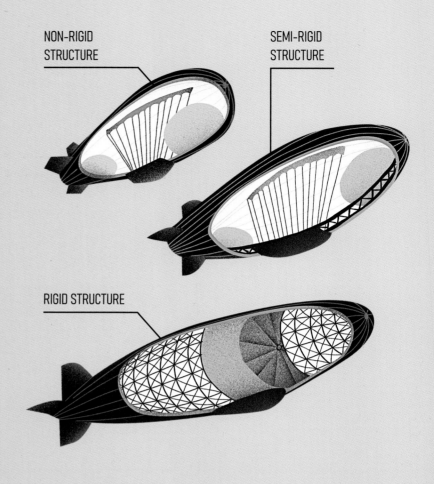

NON-RIGID STRUCTURE

SEMI-RIGID STRUCTURE

RIGID STRUCTURE

KING OF THE AIRSHIPS

Count Ferdinand von Zeppelin was not a real king but is often called the "king of airships" because of his significant contributions to airship design. Born in Germany in 1838, he served in the army for many years. After retiring at 53, he began building rigid airships. In 1900, his first airship, named LZ1, made its first flight over Lake Constance and stayed in the air for 18 minutes.

FROM MINUTES TO HOURS

The first flight was just the start. The third model, the LZ3, could stay in the air for up to 8 hours. This impressed the German army so much that they bought it from Count von Zeppelin. His later airships were designed to carry passengers and were made by the DELAG company, which von Zeppelin set up for this purpose. He also founded a shipyard, a factory for making gears used in machines, a gasworks (where gas is produced), and a factory for balloon envelopes.

FERDINAND VON ZEPPELIN

ZEPPELIN ONE, ZEPPELIN TWO ...

The letters "LZ" stand for "Luftschiff Zeppelin," which in German means "Zeppelin airship." The number shows the order in which the airships were made – first, second, third, etc. The most famous passenger-carrying airship was the LZ 127 *Graf Zeppelin*. Named after Count von Zeppelin, it was the first airship to fly around the world, completing the trip in two weeks in 1929 with paying passengers on board. The *Graf Zeppelin* also made regular flights between Germany and Brazil. During its ten years of service, it traveled over 1 million miles.

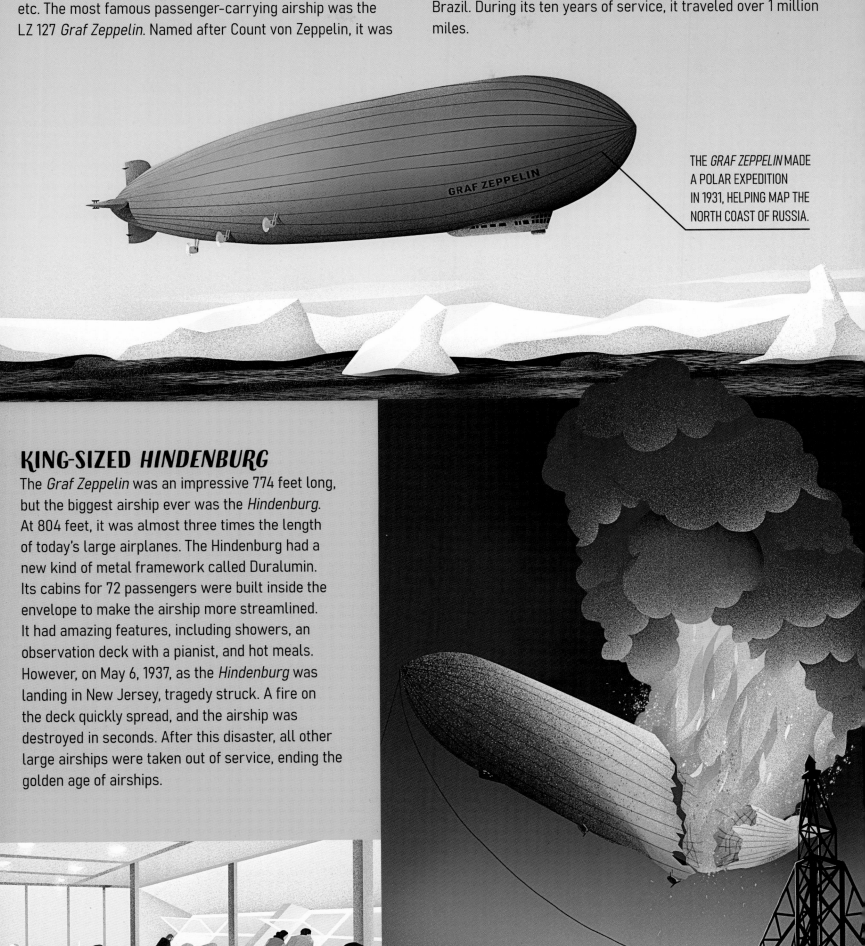

GRAF ZEPPELIN

THE *GRAF ZEPPELIN* MADE A POLAR EXPEDITION IN 1931, HELPING MAP THE NORTH COAST OF RUSSIA.

KING-SIZED *HINDENBURG*

The *Graf Zeppelin* was an impressive 774 feet long, but the biggest airship ever was the *Hindenburg*. At 804 feet, it was almost three times the length of today's large airplanes. The Hindenburg had a new kind of metal framework called Duralumin. Its cabins for 72 passengers were built inside the envelope to make the airship more streamlined. It had amazing features, including showers, an observation deck with a pianist, and hot meals. However, on May 6, 1937, as the *Hindenburg* was landing in New Jersey, tragedy struck. A fire on the deck quickly spread, and the airship was destroyed in seconds. After this disaster, all other large airships were taken out of service, ending the golden age of airships.

AIRSHIPS IN SERVICE

Airships were used for many different things. They took people and mail from place to place and were even used to explore new areas. During World War I, they were used to drop bombs and to watch over the enemy. Today, airships are popular for giving people fun sightseeing rides and sometimes help with broadcasting big sports events.

MODERN AIRSHIPS

At the motor racing event in Le Mans, France, an airship with a big Goodyear sign floats overhead. It's a semi-rigid Zeppelin NT type, made by Germany's Zeppelin Luftschifftechnik GmbH for the Goodyear company. The airship is 246 feet long and can reach speeds of up to 78 miles per hour. It features modern technology, like swiveling propellers, and can even hover in the air like a helicopter.

RUDDER

D-LZFN
ZEPPELIN

REAR WING

GOODYEAR

REAR-BALLONET AIR VENTS;
VENTS FOR THE FRONT BALLONET
ARE IN FRONT OF THE GONDOLA

MADE OF HIGH-TENACITY, ELASTIC, WATER-RESISTANT MATERIALS, THE ENVELOPE CONTAINS HELIUM (NON-FLAMMABLE), BALLONETS, AND AN ALUMINIUM FRAMEWORK.

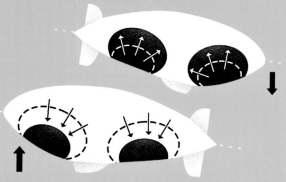

ASCENT AND DESCENT IS ACHIEVED BY ADDING AND TAKING AWAY AIR IN THE BALLONETS.

AIRSHIP CONTROL

Large airships are steered by the pilot in the front of the gondola (the basket where the crew sits). The engines control the speed, while the rudder (a flat piece at the back) helps steer the direction. When taking off or climbing, the pilot lets out heavy air from the ballonets (small compartments inside the airship) using vents (openings for air to pass through) and adjusts the rear-wing valves. To descend, the pilot lets air into the ballonets and also adjusts the rear-wing valves.

SWIVELLING PROPELLERS HELP WITH TAKING OFF, CLIMBING, AND REMAINING STATIONARY IN THE AIR.

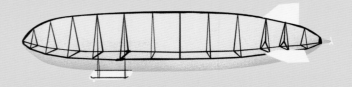

UNTIL 2014, GOODYEAR AIRSHIPS WERE NON-RIGID (BLIMPS). THE LATEST MODELS HAVE A SEMI-RIGID INNER FRAMEWORK.

INSIDE AN AIRSHIP COCKPIT

ADVANTAGES OF AIRSHIPS

Airships have a bright future because they are cheaper to operate and more eco-friendly than airplanes. They can fly for several days without needing to land, don't require airports, and can carry heavy loads to places that other vehicles can't reach.

A PROPER AIRPLANE

In the early 20th century, humans began to fly in airplanes, even though they're much, much heavier than air. The invention of the combustion engine was crucial because it provided enough power to lift the plane off the ground and keep it flying. Another key factor was learning how to handle the plane safely in the air. German inventor Otto Lilienthal made important progress by testing gliders, which helped improve airplane design and control.

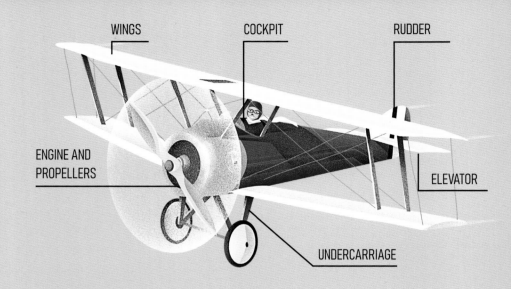

WINGS   COCKPIT   RUDDER

ENGINE AND PROPELLERS

ELEVATOR

UNDERCARRIAGE

GLIDING IN THE HEAVENS

Between 1890 and 1896, Otto Lilienthal built 18 different types of hang gliders and made countless flights with them. He and his brother Gustav created the first gliders that could fly in a controlled way for distances of up to 750 feet. Otto controlled the gliders by tilting and shifting his body, and by moving his legs in different ways. Unfortunately, in 1896, Otto crashed one of his gliders and was killed on impact.

A GLIDER ISN'T A PLANE!

The first successful airplane flight was made by American brothers Orville and Wilbur Wright. As bicycle enthusiasts, they ran a bike repair shop, which helped pay for their flying experiments. While others focused mainly on making engines stronger, the Wright brothers worked on learning how to control the plane. They were inspired by Otto Lilienthal and used their many test flights to come up with a way to steer an airplane that is still used today.

WILBUR WRIGHT

ORVILLE WRIGHT

WRIGHT CYCLE CO.

In 1903, the Wright brothers built the Wright Flyer, the first plane with a 12-horsepower engine. On December 17, in Kitty Hawk, North Carolina, they each made two successful flights. The first flight lasted just 12 seconds and covered only 120 feet, with Orville flying only 120 feet. The last flight, though, piloted by Wilbur, stayed in the air for 59 seconds and covered almost 850 feet.

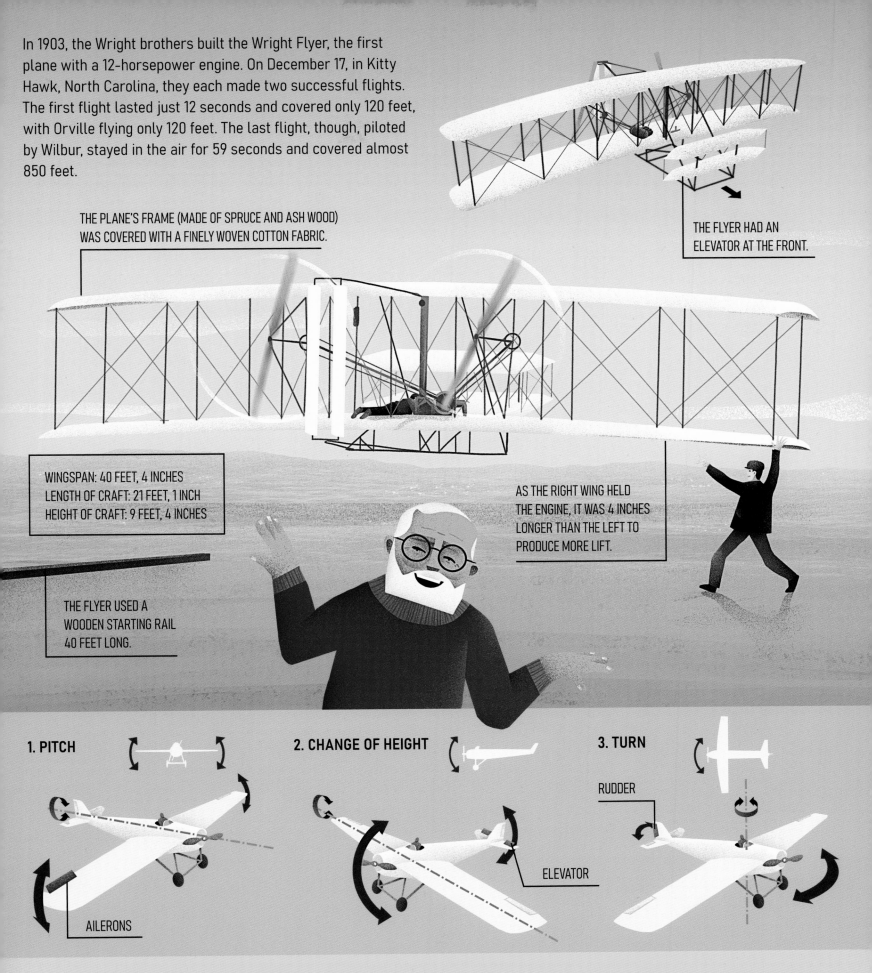

THE PLANE'S FRAME (MADE OF SPRUCE AND ASH WOOD) WAS COVERED WITH A FINELY WOVEN COTTON FABRIC.

THE FLYER HAD AN ELEVATOR AT THE FRONT.

WINGSPAN: 40 FEET, 4 INCHES
LENGTH OF CRAFT: 21 FEET, 1 INCH
HEIGHT OF CRAFT: 9 FEET, 4 INCHES

AS THE RIGHT WING HELD THE ENGINE, IT WAS 4 INCHES LONGER THAN THE LEFT TO PRODUCE MORE LIFT.

THE FLYER USED A WOODEN STARTING RAIL 40 FEET LONG.

1. PITCH

AILERONS

2. CHANGE OF HEIGHT

ELEVATOR

3. TURN

RUDDER

THREE AXES

Controlling a plane is like steering other things you already know about. When you walk, you turn your body to change direction, which is one **axis**. When you ride a bike, you turn the handlebars and lean into the turn, which uses two axes. In a plane, you use three controls to manage three directions. **Ailerons** are small parts on the wings that help the plane turn left or right by tilting the wings (much like tilting your body while biking). The **elevator** on the horizontal part of the tail changes the plane's height (up or down). And the **rudder** on the vertical part of the tail helps the plane turn and stay on course.

WARPED WINGS

The Wright Brothers' plane didn't have ailerons. Instead, the wings were designed to bend at the ends to help steer the plane. Another famous early plane, the Blériot XI, had a similar feature. French engineer Louis Blériot flew it across the English Channel on July 25, 1909. This flight was over 22 miles long and took 27 minutes. Blériot became a hero and got lots of offers to build more planes. His successful flight made people see airplane travel differently, showing it could be more than just a daring adventure for rich people.

WINGSPAN: 34 FEET
LENGTH OF CRAFT: 28 FEET
HEIGHT OF CRAFT: 8 FEET
SPEED: 66 MPH
ENGINE: 25 HORSEPOWER ANZANI

THE WINGS WERE CLEVERLY DESIGNED TO BE DETACHABLE AND PLACED ALONG THE **FUSELAGE** (THE MAIN BODY OF THE PLANE) FOR TRANSPORT.

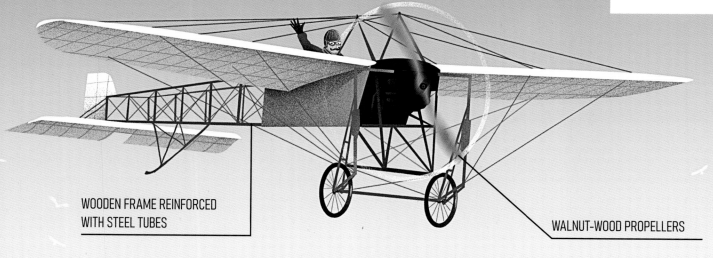

WOODEN FRAME REINFORCED WITH STEEL TUBES

WALNUT-WOOD PROPELLERS

ADRENALINE OF FLIGHT

Flying is about fun and adventure for many people. Some flyers, like American pioneer Lincoln Beachey, took it even further. Beachey was famous for his thrilling air shows with his plane, known as the "Special Looper." He amazed crowds with sharp turns, loop-the-loops, spirals, rapid descents, and even flying upside-down. His exciting races against racing cars were especially popular.

Firestone TIRES

One of the most famous triplanes was the Fokker Dr.I, which was flown by the legendary German pilot Manfred von Richthofen, also known as the Red Baron. He became the most successful pilot of World War I with this plane. The Fokker Dr.I had some challenges, like creating more air resistance and being slower during dives. But when things got tough in a fight, it could climb upward just as other planes dove down.

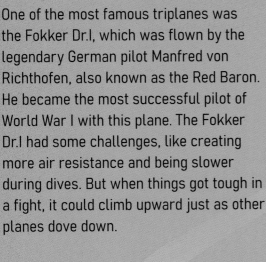

FOR ITS GUNS TO FIRE THROUGH SPINNING PROPELLERS, IT WAS FITTED WITH A SYNCHRONIZATION DEVICE INVENTED BY ANTONY FOKKER.

WINGSPAN: 28 FEET
LENGTH OF CRAFT: 19 FEET
HEIGHT OF CRAFT: 8 FEET
SPEED: 114 MPH
ENGINE: 130 HORSEPOWER CLERGET 9B

WINGSPAN (FROM THE TOP): 24 FEET; 20 FEET; 19 FEET
LENGTH OF CRAFT: 19 FEET
HEIGHT OF CRAFT: 10 FEET
SPEED: 115 MPH
ENGINE: 110 HORSEPOWER OBERURSEL UR.II

HEY, RED BARON!

SPEED AND MANEUVERABILITY

Lower speed can be a problem for a fighter plane, but the Fokker Dr.I had something special: it was really good at quick turns. The Red Baron, the famous German pilot, said his plane "climbed like a monkey and turned like a devil." During World War I, the British military created a biplane called the Sopwith Camel to counter it. This plane helped them gain an advantage, with British pilots shooting down 1,294 German planes. The most famous versions of the Sopwith Camel were the F.1 Camel and the 2F.1 Camel.

WHY WERE PLANES DOUBLE-WINGED?

Biplanes had two wings and triplanes, three wings. More wings gave these planes a bigger area to hold weight, which helped them lift off the ground more easily. Plus, the extra wings made the planes better at making quick turns. These benefits were especially important for fighter planes during World War I.

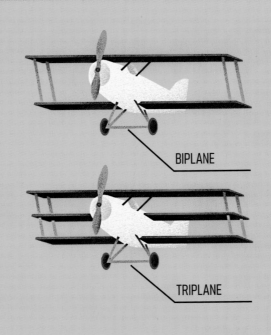

BIPLANE

TRIPLANE

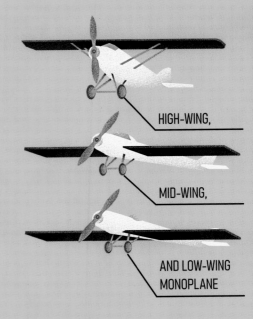

HIGH-WING,

MID-WING,

AND LOW-WING MONOPLANE

A MOMENTOUS FLIGHT

Military planes were sometimes used for other purposes. For example, the British Vickers Vimy bomber made history by completing the first non-stop flight across the Atlantic Ocean. On June 14, 1919, pilot John Alcock and navigator Arthur Brown took off from Newfoundland, Canada. The flight was challenging right from the start, as they barely cleared the treetops due to the heavy fuel load. During the journey, Brown had to climb onto the wings many times to remove ice from the control cables, and the rudder even froze completely. Despite these challenges, they stayed on course, and the ice thawed just before they landed safely in western Ireland. The flight covered 1,864 miles and took 16.5 hours.

WINGSPAN: 68 FEET
LENGTH OF CRAFT: 44 FEET
HEIGHT OF CRAFT: 16 FEET
SPEED: 103 MPH
ENGINE: 360 HORSEPOWER ROLLS-ROYCE EAGLE VIII

BRITAIN'S VICKERS VIMY BOMBER WAS FAMOUS FOR ITS MANY LONG-DISTANCE FLIGHTS.

NAVIGATOR BROWN WORKING ON THE STARBOARD WING

PILOT JOHN ALCOCK IN THE COCKPIT

LUCKY LINDY

Charles Lindbergh, who started out as an Air Mail pilot, accomplished an incredible feat by flying almost twice the distance of the Vickers Vimy flight all by himself. On May 20–21, 1927, Lindbergh spent 33.5 hours in the air in a small, simple-looking high-wing monoplane called the *Spirit of St. Louis*. He flew 3,609 miles from New York to Paris. The plane's fuselage was almost entirely filled with fuel, and Lindbergh sat so far behind the wing that he had to use a periscope to see forward. He navigated using just a compass. After the flight, Lindbergh became a hero, receiving France's Légion d'honneur, the USA's Distinguished Flying Cross, and the Medal of Honor, the country's highest military award. His achievement convinced many people that flying was the future, leading to rapid improvements in aircraft design and the beginning of international air travel.

CHARLES LINDBERGH, A.K.A. LUCKY LINDY OR LONE EAGLE

THE PLANE WAS NAMED AFTER THE CITY OF ST. LOUIS, WHICH HELPED PAY FOR IT.

WINGSPAN: 46 FEET
LENGTH OF CRAFT: 28 FEET
HEIGHT OF CRAFT: 10 FEET
SPEED: 133 MPH
ENGINE: 223 HORSEPOWER WRIGHT J-5C WHIRLWIND

WOMEN IN THE COCKPIT

In the early days of aviation, the most famous female aviator was Amelia Earhart. In 1928, she became the first woman to fly across the Atlantic, although she was the co-pilot on that flight. In 1932, she made the journey solo, completing it in 14 hours and 56 minutes. She flew in a high-wing Lockheed Vega monoplane, one of the most common transport planes in the USA at the time. Earhart also became the first female pilot to reach a speed of about 180 mph. Unfortunately, while attempting to fly around the world, she and her navigator disappeared over the Pacific Ocean. The mystery of her disappearance is only now starting to be solved.

AMELIA EARHART

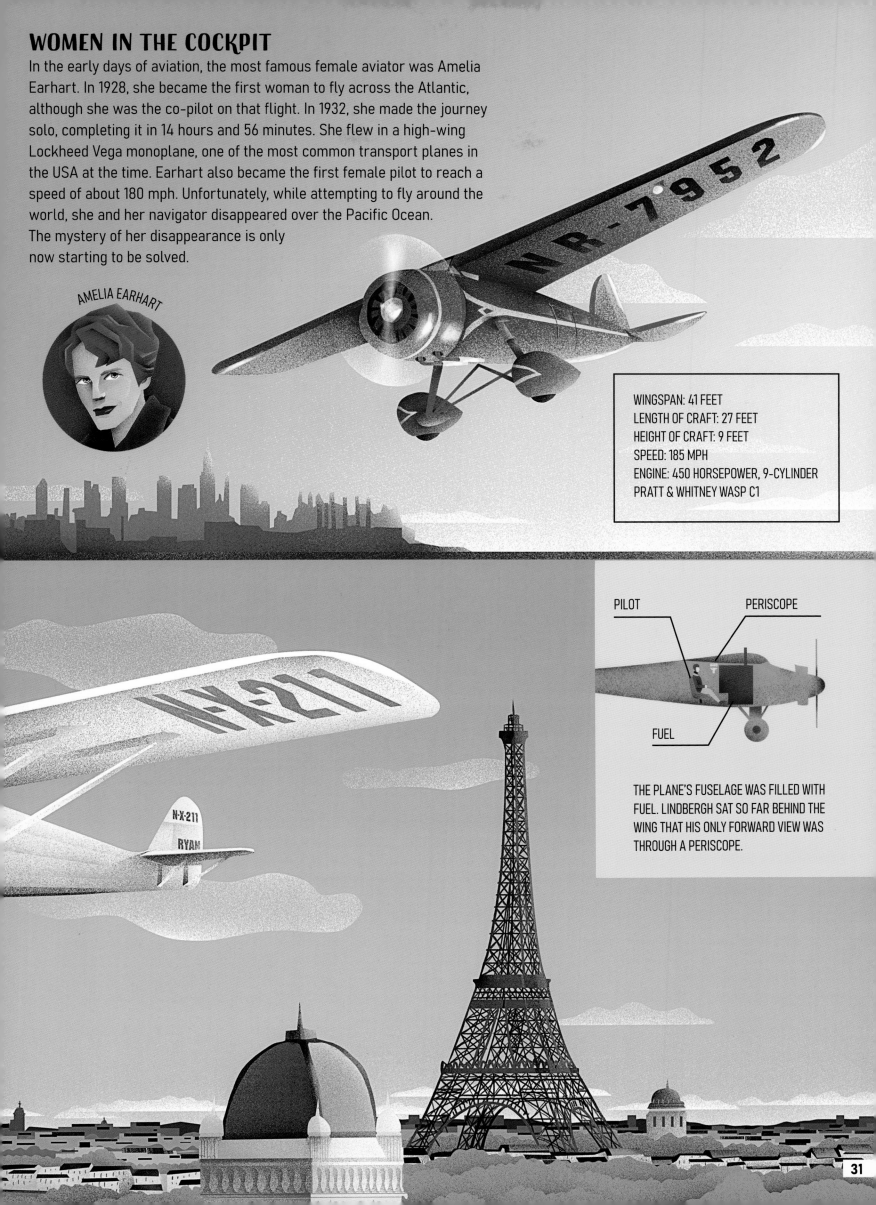

WINGSPAN: 41 FEET
LENGTH OF CRAFT: 27 FEET
HEIGHT OF CRAFT: 9 FEET
SPEED: 185 MPH
ENGINE: 450 HORSEPOWER, 9-CYLINDER
PRATT & WHITNEY WASP C1

PILOT   PERISCOPE

FUEL

THE PLANE'S FUSELAGE WAS FILLED WITH FUEL. LINDBERGH SAT SO FAR BEHIND THE WING THAT HIS ONLY FORWARD VIEW WAS THROUGH A PERISCOPE.

DANGEROUS BEGINNINGS

The first aviators had some amazing adventures, and they faced real dangers too. They took big risks to help make flying safer and better. Thanks to their bravery, we now have all kinds of incredible planes. Some of them have made history, and others are still flying today. There are not just passenger planes, but also planes used in farming, ones that are super quiet, and even planes powered by the sun.

Let's start with the Supermarine Spitfire, a famous British fighter plane that was really important during the Battle of Britain. It was made of metal and had special wings that helped it handle tough situations. There was also a naval version with folding wings and a hook to help it land safely on aircraft carriers. Even though Spitfires were retired in 1961, a few dozen are still kept flying by enthusiasts today.

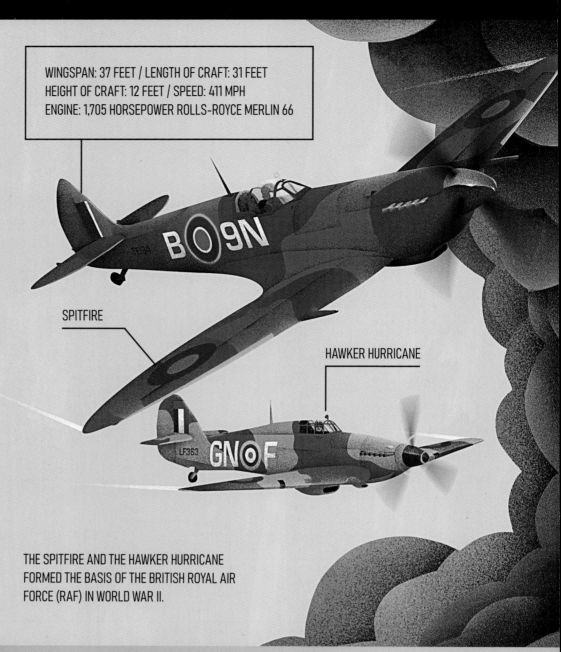

WINGSPAN: 37 FEET / LENGTH OF CRAFT: 31 FEET
HEIGHT OF CRAFT: 12 FEET / SPEED: 411 MPH
ENGINE: 1,705 HORSEPOWER ROLLS-ROYCE MERLIN 66

SPITFIRE

HAWKER HURRICANE

THE SPITFIRE AND THE HAWKER HURRICANE FORMED THE BASIS OF THE BRITISH ROYAL AIR FORCE (RAF) IN WORLD WAR II.

WINGSPAN: 36 FEET
LENGTH OF CRAFT: 27 FEET
HEIGHT OF CRAFT: 9 FEET
SPEED: 150 MPH
ENGINE: 178 HORSEPOWER
AVCO LYCOMING
O-360-F1A6

A GREAT FAVORITE

The Spitfire must be a very popular plane if people still keep it flying today. It's a beautiful plane, but in terms of popularity, it can't match the Cessna 172. This is the best-selling plane ever and has been made since 1955. The Cessna 172 has changed a lot over the years, with today's models featuring a more powerful engine and modern technology like electronic instruments and displays.

THE FIREFIGHTER CRAFT HOLDS OVER 800 GALLONS OF WATER, PLUS 35 GALLONS IN ITS FLOATS.

PLANES THAT HELP

Planes can help with all sorts of tasks. For example, they are used in farming to spread fertilizers and pesticides over fields. One of the biggest single-engine planes for this is the Air Tractor AT-802A, which is also handy for firefighting. Instead of regular wheels, it has special floats that allow it to collect water from lakes and rivers to help put out fires.

WINGSPAN: 59 FEET
LENGTH OF CRAFT: 36 FEET
HEIGHT OF CRAFT: 13 FEET
SPEED: 220 MPH
ENGINE: PRATT & WHITNEY
PT6A-67AG TURBOPROP

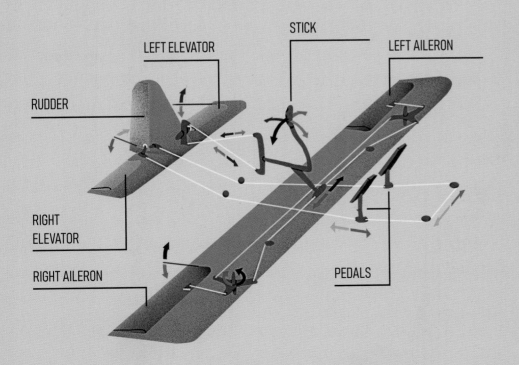

STICK

LEFT ELEVATOR

LEFT AILERON

RUDDER

RIGHT ELEVATOR

RIGHT AILERON

PEDALS

THE SECRET OF AIRCRAFT CONTROL

The pilot controls the plane using a few key tools in the cockpit. There's a yoke or stick and pedals. The yoke or stick moves back and forth to control the elevators, making the plane climb up or go down. When the yoke or the stick is moved from side to side, it controls the ailerons, which helps the plane tilt left or right. The pedals control the rudder, which steers the plane to the left or right.

SAFETY IN THE AIR

Flying in a plane is actually quite safe. One of the safest planes today is the Cirrus SR22. It has a special parachute built into it, inspired by car safety features. The inside of the Cirrus SR22 is designed for comfort, with space for 4–5 passengers. It even has cool features like charging ports for your cell phone and a display to check fuel levels, flight records, and the plane's performance. Since it started flying in 2001, the Cirrus SR22 has become one of the most popular passenger planes.

WINGSPAN: 38 FEET
LENGTH OF CRAFT: 26 FEET
HEIGHT OF CRAFT: 9 FEET
SPEED: 231 MPH
ENGINE: 310 HORSEPOWER
CONTINENTAL IO-550-N

UV TECHNOLOGY PROTECTS THE CREW FROM RADIATION IN SUNLIGHT.

UNIQUE SPECTRA LIGHTING ON THE WINGTIPS, ALSO VISIBLE IN DAYLIGHT

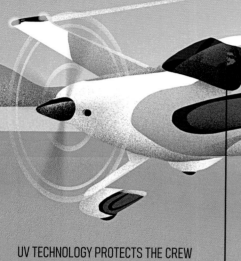

SILENT AIRPLANES

Planes with silent engines don't exist yet, but gliders don't need engines at all. They are lifted into the air by being pulled with a tow plane or a long rope and winch, similar to how a kite flies. Once in the sky, gliders use rising air currents, like a bird, to stay up. They can fly for hundreds of miles and reach speeds of over 125 mph. There are even glider competitions for the longest flight and for performing tricks.

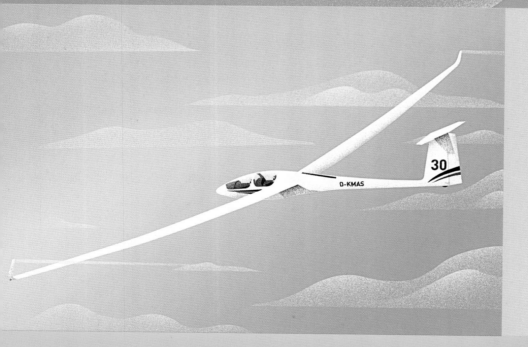

HANG-GLIDERS

A typical hang-glider has a triangular wing made of sailcloth. The pilot holds onto a crossbar that hangs from the wing. To launch, the pilot usually runs downhill to get airborne. Hang-gliders can fly for dozens or even hundreds of miles. In 2004, Angelo d'Arrigo flew a hang-glider over Mount Everest, the world's highest mountain.

DOES "RIGHT OF WAY" MEAN NOTHING TO YOU?

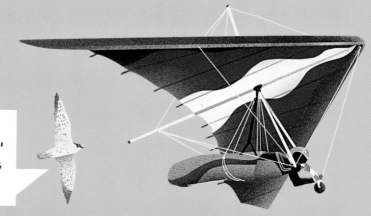

AEROBATICS

Planes can indeed perform acrobatics, which, for airplanes high up in the sky, is known as *aerobatics*. During aerobatic routines, pilots make planes do amazing tricks like loop-the-loops, sharp turns, spirals, and quick dives. One popular plane for aerobatics is the Zivko Edge 540 V3. It's made from advanced materials like carbon fiber, making it both light and strong. This plane is known for its great flying abilities, even at slower speeds.

WINGSPAN: 24 FEET
LENGTH OF CRAFT: 20 FEET
HEIGHT OF CRAFT: 8 FEET
SPEED: 265 MPH
ENGINE: 327 HORSEPOWER
LYCOMING AEIO-540-EXP

THE RED BULL AIR RACE WORLD SERIES POPULARIZED AEROBATICS TILL 2019. SINCE 2022, A WORLD CHAMPIONSHIP HAS BUILT ON THIS POPULARITY. THE ZIVKO EDGE 540 IS THE FLYERS' FAVOURITE MACHINE.

WITH THESE PLANES, SPEED, HIGH PERFORMANCE, AERODYNAMICS, AND WEIGHT ARE MOST IMPORTANT.

YOU'RE RIGHT, GRANDPA: THE EDGE IS AN AMAZING PLANE!

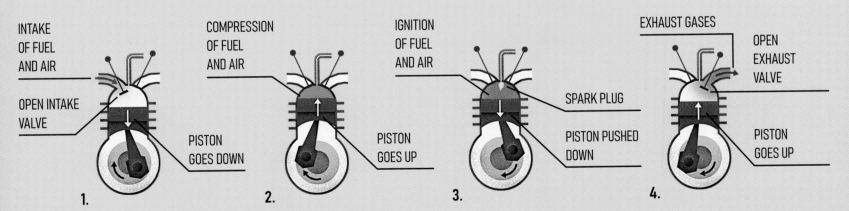

INTAKE OF FUEL AND AIR

OPEN INTAKE VALVE

PISTON GOES DOWN

1.

COMPRESSION OF FUEL AND AIR

PISTON GOES UP

2.

IGNITION OF FUEL AND AIR

SPARK PLUG

PISTON PUSHED DOWN

3.

EXHAUST GASES

OPEN EXHAUST VALVE

PISTON GOES UP

4.

ENGINES

There are two main types of engines in small planes: piston engines and jet engines. Let's focus on piston engines first. They are usually four-stroke engines, which means they go through four steps over and over. Here's how it works:

Intake Stroke: The piston moves down, pulling in a mix of fuel and air.

Compression Stroke: The piston moves up, squishing the fuel and air mixture and heating it up.

Power Stroke: A spark plug creates a spark that ignites the fuel, causing a small explosion. This explosion pushes the piston back down.

Exhaust Stroke: The piston moves up again to push out the spent gases from the engine.

This cycle keeps repeating, giving the engine power to drive the plane.

JET ENGINE

The Gulfstream G650 is a high-end private jet that offers luxury for up to 19 passengers. It features a kitchen, a bar, and a quiet cabin, making for a comfortable flying experience. As one of the largest and fastest jets in its class, it can reach speeds of up to 610 mph. It holds impressive records, including the fastest round-the-world flight at 41 hours and 7 minutes, and the longest non-stop flight at 9,650 miles.

THIS PLANE SLEEPS 10 PASSENGERS COMFORTABLY.

WINGSPAN: 100 FEET
LENGTH OF CRAFT: 100 FEET
HEIGHT OF CRAFT: 26 FEET
SPEED: 610 MPH
ENGINE: 2 ROLLS-ROYCE BR725 ENGINES

THE WINGS WERE TESTED IN A WIND TUNNEL OVER 1,400 HOURS.

ROUND-THE-WORLD FLIGHT

The Voyager was designed to fly around the world without stopping to refuel. It was the work of brilliant aerospace engineer Burt Rutan, who made his first sketch of it on a restaurant napkin over lunch in 1981. Voyager was built with ultra-modern materials, including Kevlar and carbon fiber. It performed its record-breaking circumnavigation of Earth in December 1986, covering 24,986 miles, with Dick Rutan and Jeana Yaeger sharing the piloting.

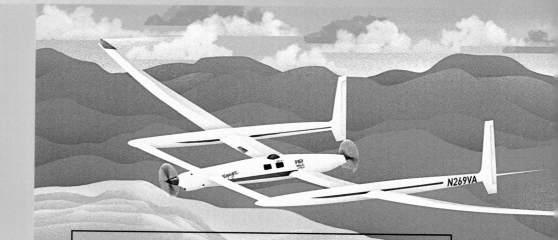

WINGSPAN: 111 FEET
LENGTH OF CRAFT: 29 FEET
HEIGHT OF CRAFT: 10 FEET
SPEED: 120 MPH
REAR ENGINE: 108 HORSEPOWER TELEDYNE CONTINENTAL VOYAGER O-200
FRONT ENGINE: 128 HORSEPOWER STANDARD CONTINENTAL O-240

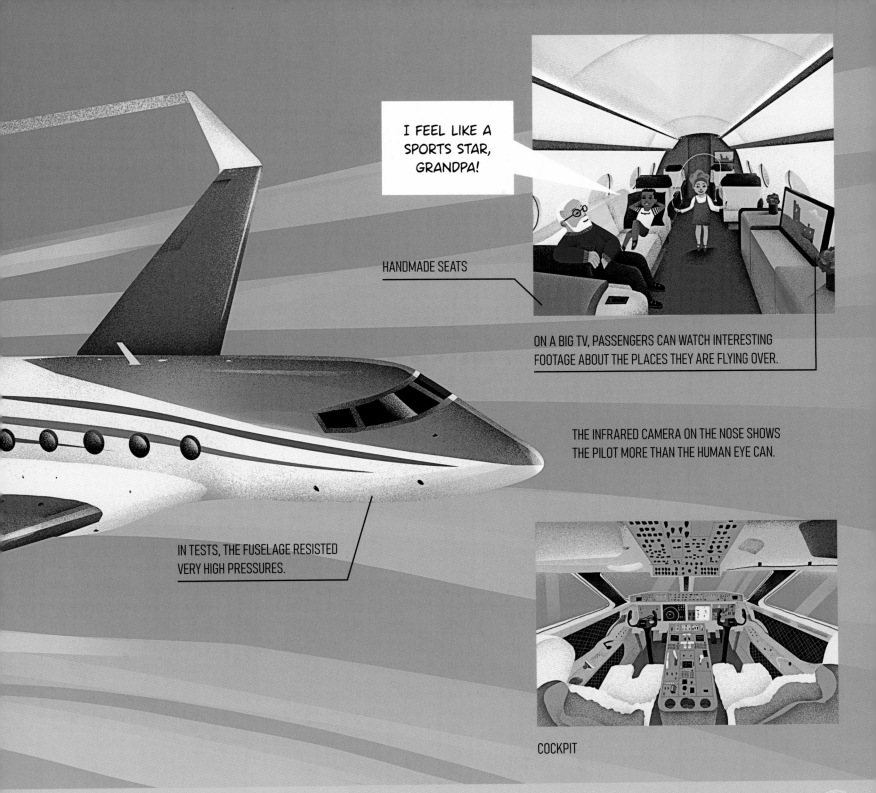

HANDMADE SEATS

ON A BIG TV, PASSENGERS CAN WATCH INTERESTING FOOTAGE ABOUT THE PLACES THEY ARE FLYING OVER.

THE INFRARED CAMERA ON THE NOSE SHOWS THE PILOT MORE THAN THE HUMAN EYE CAN.

IN TESTS, THE FUSELAGE RESISTED VERY HIGH PRESSURES.

COCKPIT

VISIONS OF THE FUTURE

The Voyager, designed by aerospace engineer Burt Rutan, was built with cutting-edge materials like Kevlar and carbon fiber. Rutan first sketched the plane on a restaurant napkin in 1981. Voyager achieved a remarkable feat in December 1986 by flying around the world without stopping to refuel. Piloted by Dick Rutan and Jeana Yeager, it covered a distance of 25,000 miles during its record-setting journey.

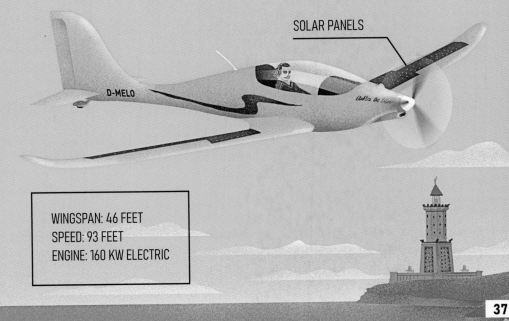

SOLAR PANELS

D-MELO

WINGSPAN: 46 FEET
SPEED: 93 FEET
ENGINE: 160 KW ELECTRIC

NOW FOR SOME BIG PLANES . . .

As air travel became safer and more popular, the need for larger planes grew. By the late 1920s, the first big airplanes, or "giants of the skies," started to appear. These early giants paved the way for today's enormous planes, which can carry hundreds of passengers and loads of several hundred tons.

WINGSPAN: 157 FEET	SPEED: 131 MPH
LENGTH OF CRAFT: 131 FEET	ENGINES: 12× CURTISS V-1570
HEIGHT OF CRAFT: 34 FEET	(EACH WITH 610 HORSEPOWER)
TAKE-OFF WEIGHT: UP TO 123,000 POUNDS	

DORNIER DO-X

One of the most fascinating planes from the past was a German flying boat from 1929. It had 12 engines and could carry 169 passengers. Despite its many technological difficulties, it was the largest and heaviest plane of its time.

THE FIRST AIRLINERS

One of the most impressive passenger planes of the 1930s was the Douglas DC-2, which first flew in 1933. Made entirely of metal and with 14 seats, it was one of the first planes to offer comfortable and reliable travel on scheduled flights. Despite Donald Douglas's initial doubts about its success, the DC-2 became a favorite among both civilian and military operators.

WINGSPAN: 85 FEET
LENGTH OF CRAFT: 62 FEET
HEIGHT OF CRAFT: 16 FEET
SPEED: 210 MPH
ENGINES: 2× WRIGHT CYCLONE
(EACH WITH 775 HORSEPOWER)

WHERE DID THE PROPELLERS GO?

Today's big planes mostly don't have propellers. Instead, they use jet engines, which became popular starting in the 1950s. Jet engines make planes much faster and allow them to fly higher, where they can avoid bad weather. This new technology made flying more reliable and led to a huge increase in the number of people traveling by plane. Commercial aviation changed forever with these advancements.

PLANES WITH JET ENGINES

The first commercial jet airliner was the British DH 106 Comet 1, which began flying passengers in 1952. At first, it was very successful, but later, problems with its design led to accidents and it had to be taken out of service. Improvements were made, and the Comet 4, an updated version, continued flying until 1997.

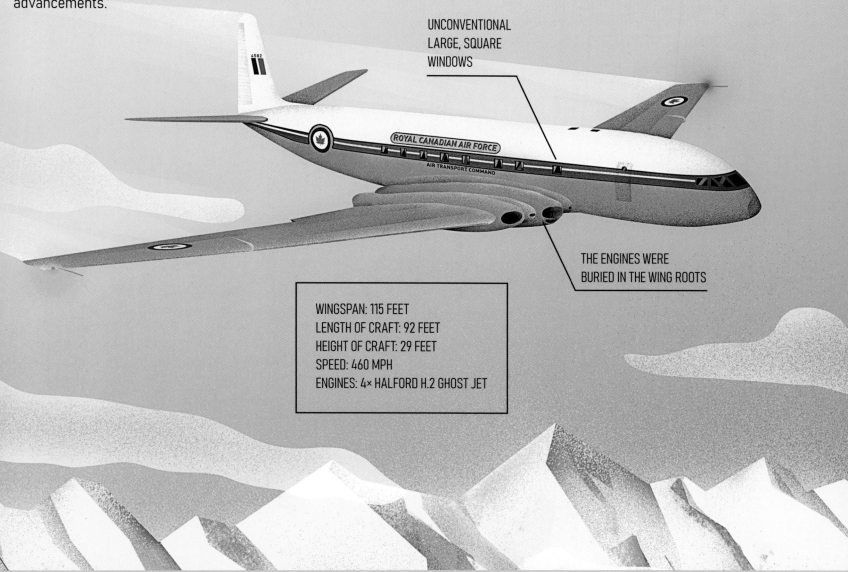

UNCONVENTIONAL LARGE, SQUARE WINDOWS

ROYAL CANADIAN AIR FORCE

AIR TRANSPORT COMMAND

THE ENGINES WERE BURIED IN THE WING ROOTS

WINGSPAN: 115 FEET
LENGTH OF CRAFT: 92 FEET
HEIGHT OF CRAFT: 29 FEET
SPEED: 460 MPH
ENGINES: 4× HALFORD H.2 GHOST JET

COMPRESSOR   BURNING FUEL

COLD AIR

TURBINE   HOT GASES SPURTING AT HIGH VELOCITY

BLOWER   COMPRESSOR   BURNING FUEL

COLD AIR   AIRFLOW BYPASS

THE SECRET OF THE JET ENGINE

A jet engine works by drawing in air through a front intake. Inside the engine, a compressor squeezes the air to make it very dense. Then, aviation fuel is added and ignited in the combustion chamber. This explosion pushes the air out of the back of the engine, creating thrust that propels the plane forward. Once the engine is started, it keeps burning fuel to keep the plane moving.

TURBOFAN JET PLANES

Most large planes at airports use what are called turbofan engines. These engines have a big fan at the front that blows air around the main engine. This extra airflow helps push the plane forward and makes it more efficient. Turbofan engines are also quieter because they mix the airstream with the exhaust gases.

PLANE WITH A BUMP

The Boeing 747, known as the jumbo jet, is famous for its unique double-decker design with a bump on top. Boeing, one of the biggest jet makers in the world, got its start by chance. William E. Boeing, who ran a timber company, saw a plane and became fascinated with flying. He learned to fly and bought a hydroplane, but after crashing it, he decided to build his own plane instead. His first plane flew in 1916, and a year later, he founded the Boeing Company.

WILLIAM EDWARD BOEING

WINGSPAN: 225 FEET
LENGTH OF CRAFT: 251 FEET
HEIGHT OF CRAFT: 64 FEET
SPEED: 570 MPH
ENGINES: 4× GENX-2B67 JET
FLYING RANGE: OVER 14,000 KM

IT CARRIES OVER 400 PASSENGERS IN THREE CLASSES. IN 1991, IT CARRIED A WORLD RECORD-BREAKING 1,122 PEOPLE DURING OPERATION SOLOMON.

747-100

747SP

747-200

747-300

747-400

747-8

THERE'S NOTHING LIKE A JUMBO

The Boeing 747 is called "jumbo" because it's enormous. It was the world's first large-volume airplane, with two decks and two aisles, making it very spacious. The bump on its nose, where the cockpit and the second deck are located, makes it easy to recognize. This giant of the skies has been flying since 1970, taking passengers on long trips around the world. However, they stopped making new ones in 2022.

Over the years, the Boeing 747 was updated and improved in several versions. It got larger and could fly farther. The newest model, the Boeing 747-8, is more fuel-efficient than the earlier 747-400 and has new wings and engines.

THE LATEST BOEINGS

The current Boeing model in production is the elegant Boeing 787 Dreamliner. Made mostly from lightweight composite materials, it's designed to be more fuel-efficient. Despite having only two engines, it can fly as far as older planes with four engines. The Dreamliner comes in three versions: the 787–8, the 787–9, and the largest, the 787–10, which can carry up to 330 passengers.

WINGSPAN: 197 FEET
LENGTH OF CRAFT: 223 FEET
HEIGHT OF CRAFT: 56 FEET
SPEED: 560 MPH
ENGINES: 2× ROLL-ROYCE TRENT 1000 JET OR GENERAL ELECTRIC GENX JET
FLYING RANGE: OVER 8,700 MILES

CHARACTERISTIC RAKED WINGTIPS

LARGE, HEAVY, YET IN THE AIR

To keep a big plane like the Dreamliner flying, its powerful engines push it forward really fast. The wings are specially shaped to help lift the plane into the air. The wings have moving parts to help with this. **Lift flaps** make the wings bigger to help the plane stay up. **Slats** let air move from below the wings to the top, which also helps with lift. **Spoilers** are used mainly during landing to slow the plane down by disrupting the airflow over the wings. All these parts work together to keep the plane flying smoothly.

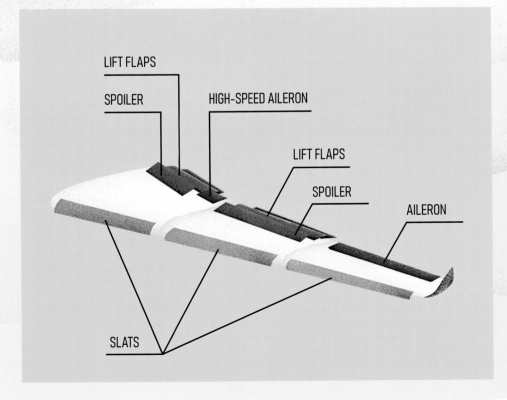

LIFT FLAPS

SPOILER

HIGH-SPEED AILERON

LIFT FLAPS

SPOILER

AILERON

SLATS

BOEING VERSUS AIRBUS

Boeing is one of the top two makers of big airplanes, and the other is Airbus, based in Europe. In 1967, France, Britain, and Germany teamed up to build a new airliner to rival Boeing's planes. They created the Airbus A300, which first flew in 1972 and started flying commercially with Air France in 1974. It took a little while for Airbus to become popular, but today, it's a world leader in making large aircraft.

IF JUMBO, WHY NOT SUPERJUMBO?

The Airbus A380, known as the Superjumbo, has been flying since 2007 and is the world's largest passenger plane. It features two full-length decks, unlike the Boeing 747, and can carry between 500 and 852 passengers. Its size required airports to update their parking, boarding bridges, and gates. Despite its massive size, it only needs a runway 300 meters shorter than other big planes for take-off and landing. However, the A380 is no longer being made, as airlines now prefer smaller, more efficient planes.

THE AIRBUS A380 HAS 4 MILLION PARTS AND IS AS TALL AS 5 GIRAFFES.

WORLD'S LARGEST

There was a plane even bigger than the Airbus A380: the Antonov An-225, a cargo plane from Ukraine. Only one was ever built, originally to carry the Buran space shuttle. It first flew in December 1988 but was retired in 1993 when the Buran program ended. After being updated, it flew again in 2011 for transporting oversized cargo and set a record for carrying the heaviest load: 253.82 tons. Sadly, it was destroyed by the Russian Army in 2022.

WINGSPAN: 290 FEET
LENGTH OF CRAFT: 276 FEET
HEIGHT OF CRAFT: 60 FEET
SPEED: 497 MPH
ENGINES: 6× PROGRESS D-18T TURBOFAN

THE TANKS IN THE WINGS HOLD UP TO 85,000 GALLONS OF FUEL.

THE AIRCRAFT HAS TWO STAIRCASES AT THE FRONT AND REAR. IT ALSO HAS TWO SMALL ELEVATORS FOR TRANSPORTING FOOD.

WINGSPAN: 80 FEET
LENGTH OF CRAFT: 240 FEET
HEIGHT OF CRAFT: 80 FEET
SPEED: 587 MPH
ENGINES: 4× GP7270 JET, OR
4X TRENT 970/B OR 972/B JET
FLYING RANGE: OVER 9,300 MILES

THIS PLANE PROVIDES LUXURY 1ST CLASS TRAVEL. MOST PASSENGERS SLEEP ON RECLINING SEATS, ALTHOUGH PRIVATE CABINS WITH A LARGE BED AND SHOWER FACILITIES ARE AVAILABLE.

ALL COCKPIT CONTROLS ARE DIGITAL. THERE ISN'T EVEN A JOYSTICK, LET ALONE DIALS.

ANOTHER GIANT

The Stratolaunch carrier aircraft is another giant in the skies. Built to launch rockets into space, it has two fuselages and the world's largest wingspan, stretching an incredible 384 feet. The cockpit is in the right-side fuselage, while the left-side fuselage holds the flight-recording systems. Still in the testing phase, it has made two short flights since 2019 and will eventually be used to test hypersonic aircraft.

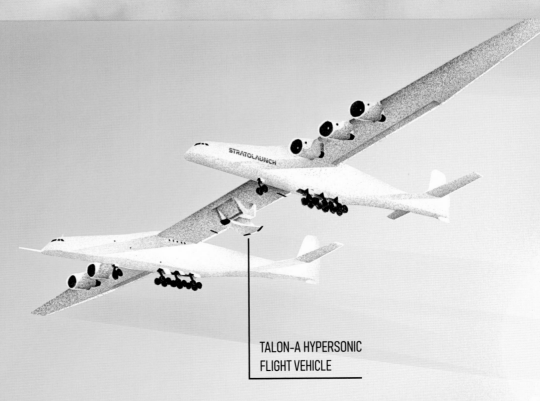

TALON-A HYPERSONIC FLIGHT VEHICLE

FASTER THAN SOUND

Now, let's dive into the world of the fastest planes: the supersonic ones. Supersonic planes travel faster than the speed of sound – about 767 miles per hour. Thanks to advances in aerodynamics and powerful engines, these planes can reach incredible speeds. Imagine flying from London to New York in just 3 hours! However, supersonic flight has some drawbacks, including high costs, harmful emissions, and a loud noise called a sonic boom. Because of these issues, supersonic aircraft are mainly used by the military today.

BATTLING WITH SPEED

It took thousands of years for people to learn to fly, and in just 50 years, they reached incredible speeds! One of the first planes to break the sound barrier was the Bell X-1, which did so on October 14, 1947, reaching a speed of 806 miles per hour. Its design was inspired by the shape of a bullet, which helps with stability at such high speeds. The X-1 used so much fuel that its record-setting flight only lasted five minutes. To make it to the sky, it was carried and launched from under the wings of a B-29 bomber. After running out of fuel, pilot Chuck Yeager glided the X-1 to a safe landing on a dry lake bed.

WINGSPAN: 28 FEET
LENGTH OF CRAFT: 30 FEET
HEIGHT OF CRAFT: 10 FEET
SPEED: 957 MPH
ENGINE: Reaction Motors XLR11-RM3 rocket

FASTEST OF THE FAST

Imagine flying at over 4,300 miles per hour! That was the speed of the North American X-15, an experimental plane that reached 4,520 miles per hour in 1967 – a record that still stands today. The X-15 flew so high that it almost reached outer space, so it had a special skin made of nickel and aluminum to handle temperatures up to 1500°F. The X-15 helped us learn not only about building faster airplanes and spacecraft but also about how people cope with extreme speeds and conditions, which is crucial for space travel.

WINGSPAN: 23 FEET / LENGTH OF CRAFT: 50 FEET
HEIGHT OF CRAFT: 14 FEET / SPEED: 4,520 MPH
ENGINE: REACTION MOTORS XLR99-RM-2 LIQUID-PROPELLANT ROCKET

FROM EXPERIMENT TO REALITY

At first, all the fast planes were experimental. Later, some of them were used in the military and for other purposes. One of the most famous military aircraft was the Lockheed SR-71 Blackbird from the USA. In 1976, it reached an incredible speed of 2,192 miles per hour. Made mostly of titanium, the Blackbird could handle temperatures up to 575°F at such high speeds. It also had special technology to avoid detection by radar, making it hard for enemies to spot. Because of its extreme speed, it was out of range of most missiles and was never shot down during its service.

WINGSPAN: 55 FEET
LENGTH OF CRAFT: 107 FEET
HEIGHT OF CRAFT: 18 FEET
SPEED: 2,195 MPH
ENGINES: 2× PRATT & WHITNEY
J58-1 AXIAL FLOW TURBOJET
WITH AFTERBURNER

IT WAS NAMED "BLACKBIRD" BECAUSE OF ITS DARK COLOR.

U.S. AIRFORCE

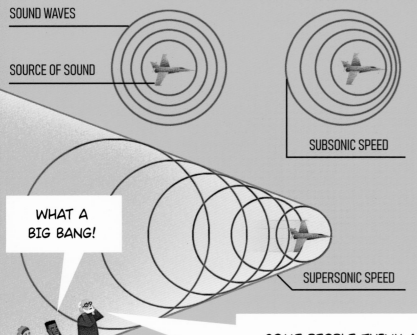

SOUND WAVES

SOURCE OF SOUND

SUBSONIC SPEED

WHAT A BIG BANG!

SUPERSONIC SPEED

SONIC BOOM

Sound travels in waves through the air. How fast it moves depends on which material it's traveling through. We measure sound speed with something called Mach numbers. Mach 1 is the speed of sound, which is about 767 miles per hour in the air. When a plane flies faster than this, it makes a **sonic boom** – a really loud noise that can even break windows. This happens because the plane creates a shock wave that looks like a cone behind it. To avoid problems on the ground, planes that fly this fast are usually only allowed to do so at high altitudes or over the ocean. Thunder is an example of a sonic boom from nature.

SOME PEOPLE THINK A SONIC BOOM OCCURS ONLY AS THE SOUND BARRIER IS BEING BROKEN. BUT IT LASTS FOR THE WHOLE SUPERSONIC FLIGHT!

GREAT DESIGN

Airliners don't fly quite that fast. The famous British-French Concorde was the closest, reaching speeds of about 1,354 miles per hour. It looked very futuristic and even won a design award. Sixteen Concordes were built, and they mostly flew with Air France and British Airways starting in 1976.

THERE BEFORE YOU KNOW IT!

The Concorde was so fast that passengers barely had time for a meal! The plane's high speed put a lot of stress on its all-metal structure. Because of the intense heat from flying so fast, Concorde's metal body expanded by 8 inches at full speed.

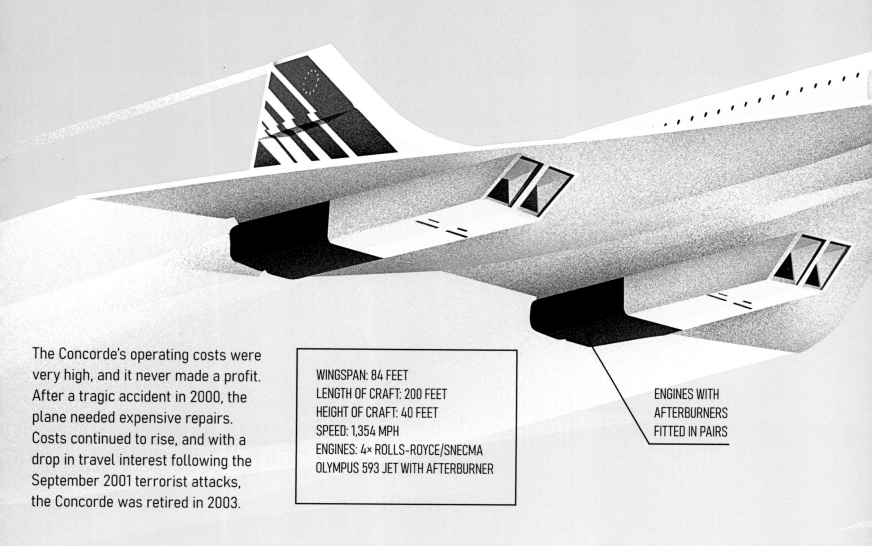

The Concorde's operating costs were very high, and it never made a profit. After a tragic accident in 2000, the plane needed expensive repairs. Costs continued to rise, and with a drop in travel interest following the September 2001 terrorist attacks, the Concorde was retired in 2003.

WINGSPAN: 84 FEET
LENGTH OF CRAFT: 200 FEET
HEIGHT OF CRAFT: 40 FEET
SPEED: 1,354 MPH
ENGINES: 4× ROLLS-ROYCE/SNECMA
OLYMPUS 593 JET WITH AFTERBURNER

ENGINES WITH AFTERBURNERS FITTED IN PAIRS

TOO NOISY

The Concorde was so loud at take-off that it could be heard from 5 miles away. Because of this noise, it wasn't allowed to fly out of many airports. The plane mainly flew across the ocean between Paris or London and New York. With space for up to 128 passengers, it could make the trip in half the time of other planes. The fastest flight ever recorded was from New York to London, taking just 2 hours, 52 minutes, and 59 seconds.

THE COCKPIT TILTED ON LANDING AND TAKE-OFF TO ALLOW PILOTS TO SEE THE RUNWAY.

ON TAKE-OFF, THE TAIL WAS PROTECTED BY A RETRACTABLE BUMPER WHEEL.

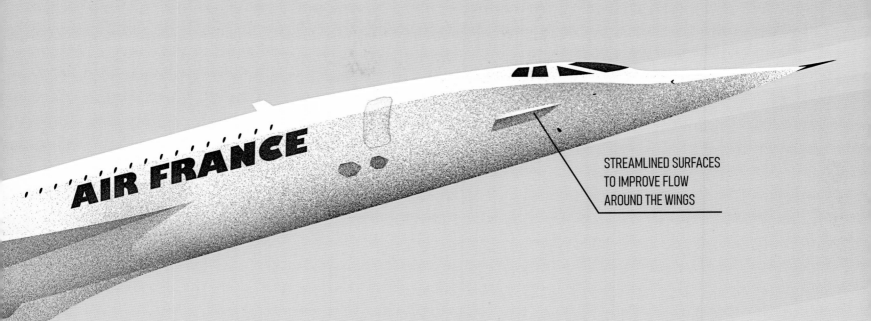

AIR FRANCE

STREAMLINED SURFACES
TO IMPROVE FLOW
AROUND THE WINGS

MIGHT THE CONCORDE RETURN?

The Concorde might not fly again, but there are new projects working on similar planes. These projects aim to solve the problem of the loud sonic boom, making it quieter, like the sound of a car door closing. They also plan to make these planes cheaper and more eco-friendly. The goal is to create a plane that flies four times faster than the speed of sound.

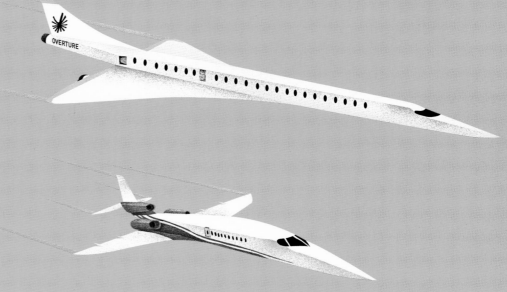

ALMIGHTY HELICOPTERS

We're nearing the end, but we haven't quite reached it yet. Lastly, we'll explore helicopters – machines that can hover, take off, land vertically, and even fly backwards, thanks to their rotors on top. While helicopters don't fly as fast as airplanes (their top speed is about 174 mph) and have a shorter flight range, they are still incredibly important. Their unique abilities make them essential in many situations.

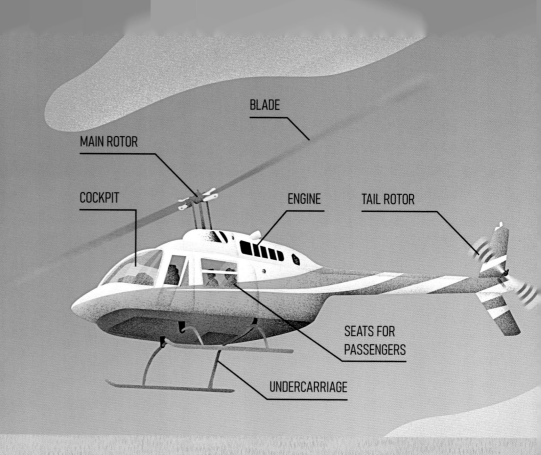

BLADE

MAIN ROTOR

COCKPIT

ENGINE

TAIL ROTOR

SEATS FOR PASSENGERS

UNDERCARRIAGE

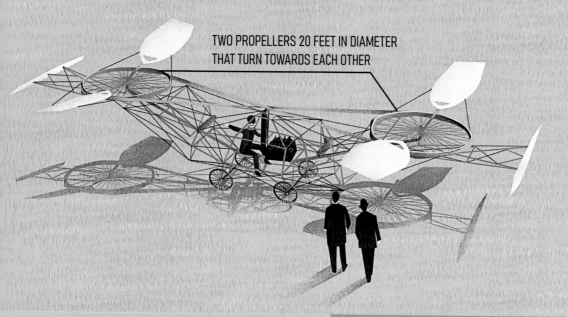

TWO PROPELLERS 20 FEET IN DIAMETER THAT TURN TOWARDS EACH OTHER

THE FIRST HELICOPTER

Leonardo da Vinci once sketched an idea for a helicopter, called an "aerial screw." It took over 300 years for this idea to become a real working machine. The first successful helicopter flight was made by French engineer Paul Cornu on November 13, 1907. His machine, which looked like an insect, managed to lift off the ground and stay in the air for 20 seconds.

A RECORD-BREAKING HELICOPTER

The Focke-Wulf Fw 61 made a big leap in helicopter history. Its first flight on June 26, 1936 lasted only 28 seconds, but within a year, it set several records. It climbed to a height of 8,000 feet, stayed in the air for 1 hour and 29 minutes, covered a distance of 50 miles, and reached an average speed of 76 miles per hour.

TWO COUNTER-ROTATING ROTORS 7 METRES IN DIAMETER

D-EKRA

SMALL PROPELLER ON THE NOSE

AIRPLANE FUSELAGE OF THE FW-44 STIEGLITZ

AIRPLANE OR HELICOPTER?

The Focke-Wulf Fw 61 may not look like the helicopters we see today, but it was an important step in their development. It was a mix of an airplane and a helicopter. The first helicopters as we know them were designed by Igor Sikorsky, an aviation pioneer from Ukraine who later moved to the USA in 1919. Sikorsky focused on creating helicopters and founded the Sikorsky Aircraft company, which is still a major helicopter manufacturer today. His first major breakthrough was the Vought-Sikorsky VS-300, which flew for the first time on May 13, 1940. The VS-300 initially had no metal covering and was still perfecting its tail rotor design. Although the idea of having three rotors was considered, it ultimately used just one main rotor.

LENGTH OF CRAFT: 28 FEET
HEIGHT OF CRAFT: 10 FEET
ROTOR DIAMETER: 30 FEET
SPEED: 120 MPH
TAKE-OFF WEIGHT: 1,150 FEET
ENGINE POWER: 90 HORSEPOWER

IGOR SIKORSKY

SIKORSKY'S HOVERFLY

Four years later, the Sikorsky R-4 helicopter was built in large numbers. It had been tested in tough places like Alaska and Burma and was updated with a more powerful engine and a new type of propeller. Out of the 131 R-4 helicopters made, 100 went to the British Royal Air Force, where they were called "Hoverfly."

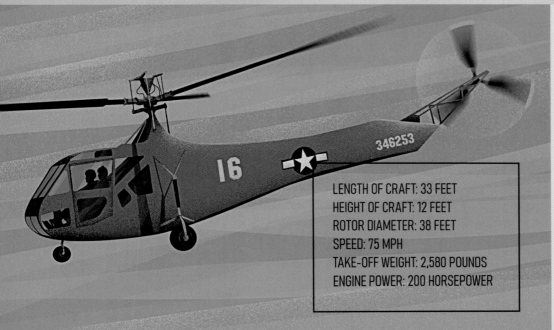

LENGTH OF CRAFT: 33 FEET
HEIGHT OF CRAFT: 12 FEET
ROTOR DIAMETER: 38 FEET
SPEED: 75 MPH
TAKE-OFF WEIGHT: 2,580 POUNDS
ENGINE POWER: 200 HORSEPOWER

A HELICOPTER WITH MUSCLES

After Sikorsky's death, his team developed the Sikorsky UH-60 Black Hawk, which won a competition to find a new utility helicopter for the United States Army. The Black Hawk has been in use since 1979. This powerful helicopter can carry up to 2,645 pounds on board and up to 9,000 pounds as suspended cargo. It has been used for rescue missions, air strikes, and transporting up to eleven fully armed troops.

LENGTH OF CRAFT: 65 FEET / HEIGHT OF CRAFT: 17 FEET
ROTOR DIAMETER: 54 FEET / TAKE-OFF WEIGHT: 23,500 POUNDS
ENGINES: 2× GENERAL ELECTRIC T700-GE-701C TURBOSHAFT, EACH WITH 1,890 HORSEPOWER

HELICOPTER CONTROL

The cockpit of a helicopter looks similar to that of an airplane, but flying a helicopter is trickier. This is because helicopters experience something called "dissymmetry of lift" – big words that just mean moving one way while being pushed the other way. Just imagine swimming in one direction and then a sudden rush of water moves you in another. To keep the helicopter from spinning, it usually has a smaller rotor at the end of its tail to help balance it out.

To fly a helicopter, the pilot uses three controls: the **cyclic stick** to steer, the **pedals** to prevent spinning and guide direction, and the **collective lever** to control altitude (how high up you are) by adjusting the rotor blades. The **throttle**, found on the collective lever, adjusts engine power for climbing or descending.

The cyclic stick tilts the rotor disk to control direction. Moving the stick forward makes the helicopter go forward, while shifting it to the right makes it turn right.

The direction of flight is controlled by the pedals, which rotate the tail rotor blades.

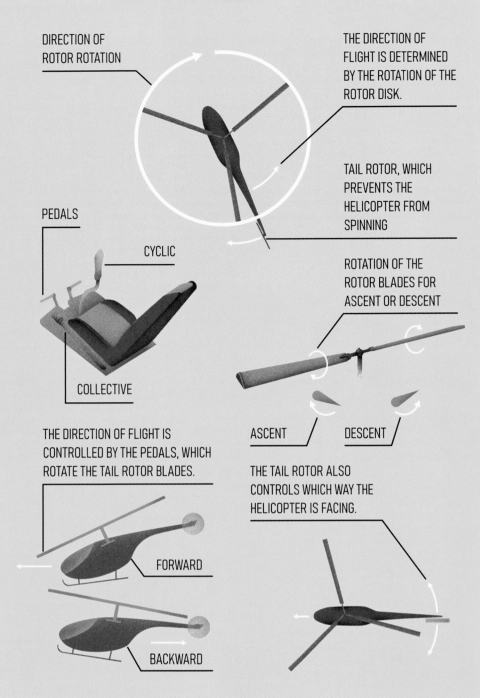

DIRECTION OF ROTOR ROTATION

THE DIRECTION OF FLIGHT IS DETERMINED BY THE ROTATION OF THE ROTOR DISK.

TAIL ROTOR, WHICH PREVENTS THE HELICOPTER FROM SPINNING

PEDALS

CYCLIC

COLLECTIVE

ROTATION OF THE ROTOR BLADES FOR ASCENT OR DESCENT

ASCENT   DESCENT

THE DIRECTION OF FLIGHT IS CONTROLLED BY THE PEDALS, WHICH ROTATE THE TAIL ROTOR BLADES.

THE TAIL ROTOR ALSO CONTROLS WHICH WAY THE HELICOPTER IS FACING.

FORWARD

BACKWARD

EVACUATION CARRIERS

A HELICOPTER PILOT'S LICENSE

Being a helicopter pilot is really hard. In 1946, the Bell 47 became the first helicopter approved for ordinary people to use, and it was produced in large numbers. It was also useful in the military for evacuating injured people. From 1961, it even helped train astronauts on the Apollo program to use the lunar lander.

LENGTH OF CRAFT: 32 FEET
HEIGHT OF CRAFT: 9 FEET
ROTOR DIAMETER: 37 FEET
TAKE-OFF WEIGHT: MAX. 2,953 POUNDS
ENGINE: 286 HORSEPOWER
LYCOMING TVO-435-F1A

BIG COPTER, LITTLE COPTER

Helicopters come in different sizes, and we can group them based on things like the number of engines, rotor type, what they're used for, and their weight. One common way to sort them is by how much weight they can carry while flying. This includes the helicopter itself, fuel, crew, and any load. Ultralight helicopters weigh up to 1,300 pounds, light ones up to 5,500 pounds, medium ones up to 17,600 pounds, heavy ones over 17,600 pounds, and superheavy ones over 55,000 pounds.

THE US ROBINSON R44 HAS A MAXIMUM TAKE-OFF WEIGHT OF 1,134 KG. BECAUSE OF ITS LOW PRICE AND CHEAPNESS TO RUN, IT IS THE WORLD'S TOP-SELLING HELICOPTER.

THE RUSSIAN SUPERHEAVY MIL MI-26 IS THE WORLD'S HEAVIEST HELICOPTER. ITS MAXIMUM TAKE-OFF WEIGHT IS OVER 120,000 POUNDS.

LENGTH OF CRAFT: 32 FEET
HEIGHT OF CRAFT: 9 FEET
ROTOR DIAMETER: 35 FEET
TAKE-OFF WEIGHT: MAX. 3,527 POUNDS
ENGINE: 530 (REDUCED TO 360)
HORSEPOWER TURBOMECA ARTOUSTE
IIC6 TURBOSHAFT

RESCUE HELICOPTER

Aviation pioneer Igor Sikorsky once said, "The helicopter's role in saving lives represents one of the most glorious pages in the history of human flight." British researchers found that one helicopter is as useful as 17 ambulances. It can rescue people from mountains, battlefields, or accident scenes. In July 1956, the French Aerospatiale SA-313 Alouette II became the first helicopter to perform a mountain rescue, saving a climber at 13,000 feet. A year later, it rescued the crew of a crashed Sikorsky S-58 from Mont Blanc.

THE AEROSPATIALE SA-313 ALOUETTE II WAS THE FIRST MASS-PRODUCED HELICOPTER WITH A JET ENGINE.

KINDS OF ROTORS

Large helicopters often have two main rotors. These can be different types: **coaxial**, where the rotors are stacked on top of each other; **intermeshing**, where the rotors overlap; and **quadcopters**, with four rotors. Two of the most notable types are **tandem** and **transverse** rotors.

ALL ABOARD, TROOPS!

The legendary Boeing CH-47 Chinook is a tandem-rotor helicopter. Since its first flight on September 21, 1961, it has been used in many tough combat situations, mainly to move troops and deliver supplies on the battlefield. It can carry up to 55 troops or a 28,000-pound load. It features a loading ramp at the rear and three external cargo hooks. For its size, it has an impressive top speed of 195 mph.

CONVERTIPLANE

The Bell Boeing V-22 Osprey is a unique **convertiplane**, which means it combines the features of a helicopter and an airplane. It can take off and land vertically like a helicopter, thanks to its rotors, but it also has the speed and range of a fixed-wing aircraft. This mix of features makes it very adaptable.

The Bell and Boeing companies worked together to create the V-22 Osprey. It first flew in 1989 but wasn't used until 2007. The time spent developing it paid off. The Osprey can fold its rotors and wings in 90 seconds, making it more compact. It can fly at speeds of up to 350 mph and has a range of about 1,000 miles – or 2,175 miles with extra fuel tanks. It can carry 32 troops or up to 20,000 pounds of cargo inside and 15,000 pounds of cargo outside.

FOLDING ROTORS

FOLD-IN WINGS

LENGTH OF CRAFT: 57 FEET / HEIGHT OF CRAFT: 22 FEET
ROTOR DIAMETER: 39 FEET / WINGSPAN: 46 FEET
TAKE-OFF WEIGHT: MAX. 47,400 POUNDS
ENGINE: 2× T406/AE 1107C-LIBERTY TURBOSHAFT, EACH WITH OVER 6,000 HORSEPOWER

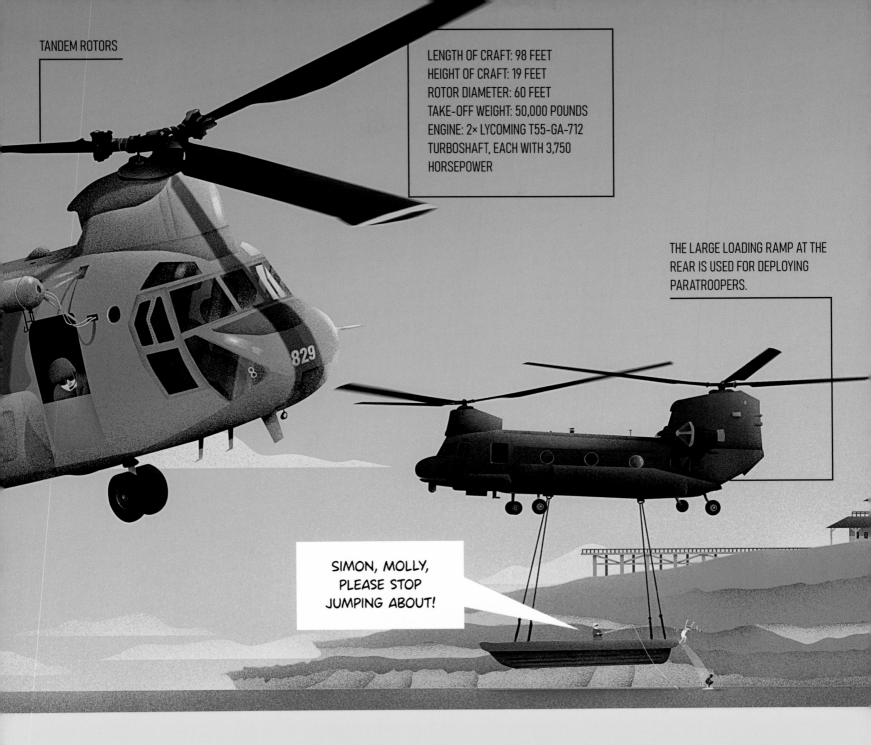

TANDEM ROTORS

LENGTH OF CRAFT: 98 FEET
HEIGHT OF CRAFT: 19 FEET
ROTOR DIAMETER: 60 FEET
TAKE-OFF WEIGHT: 50,000 POUNDS
ENGINE: 2× LYCOMING T55-GA-712
TURBOSHAFT, EACH WITH 3,750
HORSEPOWER

THE LARGE LOADING RAMP AT THE
REAR IS USED FOR DEPLOYING
PARATROOPERS.

SIMON, MOLLY,
PLEASE STOP
JUMPING ABOUT!

REALITY OR SCI-FI?

The Osprey looks like something from
a sci-fi movie. Designers have big
imaginations, and the helicopters of the
future will look even more futuristic.
They'll use the latest materials and
technology to keep costs low and
make them work better. Just like
with airplanes, more and more future
helicopters will be unmanned and
operated by computers.

THE NORTHROP GRUMMAN
MQ-8 IS AN UNMANNED
HELICOPTER USED FOR
RECONNAISSANCE,
SURVEILLANCE, RESEARCH,
AND LASER TARGETING OF
OBJECTS ON THE GROUND.

PROTOTYPE OF THE SIKORSKY S-97
RAIDER, WHICH WILL REACH SPEEDS
OF 273 MPH AND BE ABLE TO
OPERATE WITHOUT A PILOT.

THAT'S ALL, FOLKS!

With so much interesting information, I'll bet your head feels as big as a hot-air balloon!

So, to keep things clear, here's a quick recap of the most important bits.

NOVEMBER 21, 1783

FIRST FREE BALLOON FLIGHT, MADE BY JEAN-FRANÇOIS PILÂTRE DE ROZIER AND FRANÇOIS D'ARLANDE

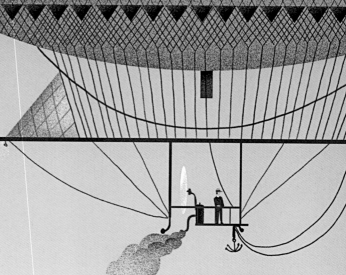

EARLY 16TH CENTURY

LEONARDO DA VINCI DESIGNS THE ORNITHOPTER AND INVENTS THE AERIAL SCREW AND THE PRINCIPLE OF THE PARACHUTE

ICARUS

875

FIRNAS'S FLIGHT BY GLIDER

CHINESE PAPER KITES

1782

MONTGOLFIER BROTHERS INVENT THE HOT-AIR BALLOON

SEPTEMBER 24, 1852

HENRI GIFFARD'S FIRST CONTROLLED AIRSHIP FLIGHT

| 1500 | 1000 | 500 | | 500 | 1000 | 1500 | 1600 | 1700 | 1800 | 1850 |

BEFORE THE COMMON ERA | COMMON ERA

LU-BAN
507–444 BCE

ABBAS IBN FIRNAS
810–887

JOSEPH-MICHEL MONTGOLFIER
1740–1810

HENRI GIFFARD
1825–1882

MOZI
470–391 BCE

LEONARDO DA VINCI
1452–1519

JACQUES ÈTIENNE MONTGOLFIER
1745–1799

FERDINAND VON ZEPPELIN
1838–1917

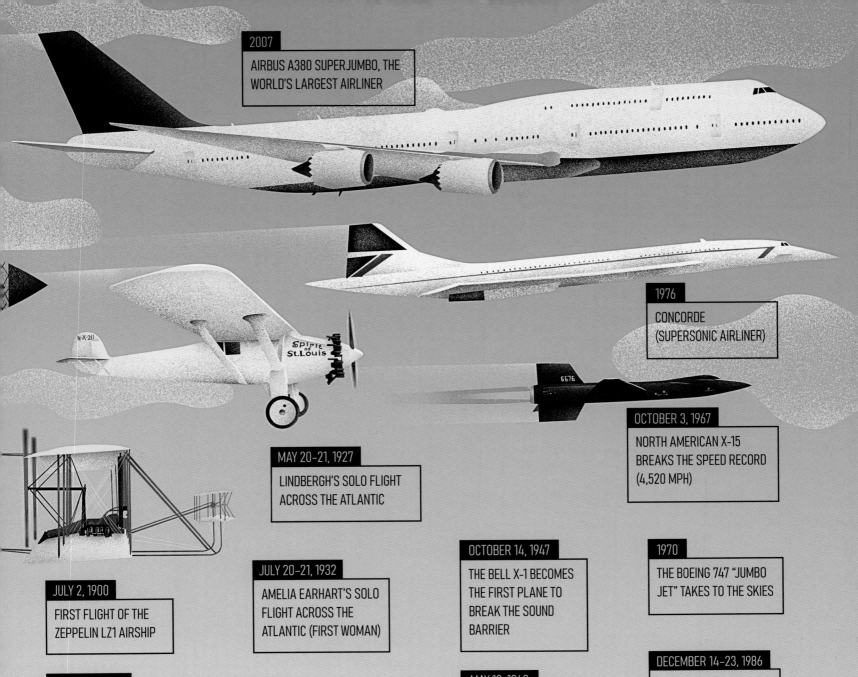

2007
AIRBUS A380 SUPERJUMBO, THE WORLD'S LARGEST AIRLINER

1976
CONCORDE (SUPERSONIC AIRLINER)

MAY 20–21, 1927
LINDBERGH'S SOLO FLIGHT ACROSS THE ATLANTIC

OCTOBER 3, 1967
NORTH AMERICAN X-15 BREAKS THE SPEED RECORD (4,520 MPH)

OCTOBER 14, 1947
THE BELL X-1 BECOMES THE FIRST PLANE TO BREAK THE SOUND BARRIER

1970
THE BOEING 747 "JUMBO JET" TAKES TO THE SKIES

JULY 20–21, 1932
AMELIA EARHART'S SOLO FLIGHT ACROSS THE ATLANTIC (FIRST WOMAN)

JULY 2, 1900
FIRST FLIGHT OF THE ZEPPELIN LZ1 AIRSHIP

DECEMBER 14–23, 1986
VOYAGER FLIES AROUND THE GLOBE WITHOUT STOPPING OR REFUELING

AUGUST 9, 1884
LA FRANCE IS THE FIRST AIRSHIP TO COMPLETE A ROUNDTRIP

DECEMBER 17, 1903
FIRST FLIGHT OF THE WRIGHT BROTHERS' FLYER

MAY 13, 1940
VOUGHT-SIKORSKY VS-300, THE FIRST TRUE HELICOPTER

1900   1950   2000

WILBUR WRIGHT
1867–1912

WILLIAM EDWARD BOEING
1881–1956

IGOR SIKORSKY
1889–1972

ORVILLE WRIGHT
1871–1948

AMELIA EARHART
1897–1937

CHARLES LINDBERGH
1902–1974

THANKS, KIDS FOR SOARING THROUGH THIS ADVENTURE IN FLIGHT WITH SUCH ENTHUSIASM. UNTIL NEXT TIME, KEEP YOUR CURIOSITY FLYING HIGH!

ABOUT THIS BOOK

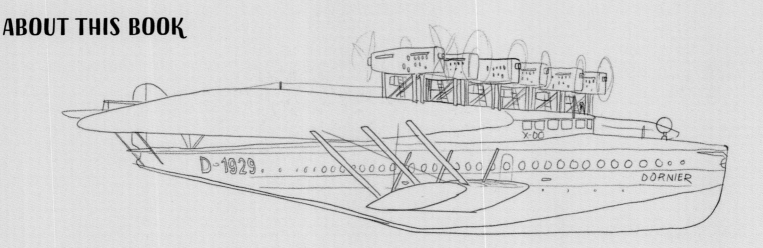

Summer 1981, end of the school year. A proud first-grader, I show my grandmother the big "A" on my report card. She rewards me with an ice cream and a book. I fall in love with the book – not because of the subject, though, but because of my name in the title: *Tommy's Discoveries*. Everything that Tommy in the book goes through, I go through alongside him. The memory has remained so sharp that when I got a chance to write a children's book of my own, I wanted to give my readers the same feeling. On opening my book, he, she, or they are welcomed by Grandpa Edward, so becoming part of the adventure.

In 1993, I was waiting at Frankfurt Airport for a flight to New York with my friends from the Czech national baseball team, about to fly for the first time. I'd never been more nervous. But when I laid eyes on the double-decker Boeing, my nervousness gave way to awe. I'll never forget the size of the thing, the take-off forcing me back in my seat, and the landing at the second attempt (the pilot got it wrong the first time around). As you see, I didn't have to search very hard to find a subject for my book.

At first, however, I was unsure where to begin and how to go about it. Czech writer Zdeněk Svěrák once remarked that when he writes for children, he gets down on his knees to see the world from a child's perspective. I opted for this approach. I used social media to ask parents to find out what interests their children most about flying. In this way, I gathered lots of questions and suggestions that have helped me see my subject through a child's eyes.

To find answers to what most interests children, I had to do my research. I read books with titles like *The Aircraft Book: The Definitive Visual History*, *An Encyclopaedia of Modern Aircraft*, *How Airliners Fly*, *Ask the Pilot*, and even *Myths and Legends of Ancient Greece*. I searched the internet for interesting stories about aircraft and people who developed them. I discovered many more interesting things than I was able to include in this book. But all the most interesting stuff is here.

I'm confident that young readers will enjoy this book. What's more, I trust that some will be inspired to explore the subject and take the adventure further. Who knows? Maybe they are the pilots and aircraft designers of the future!

Tomáš SMOT Svoboda, a.k.a. Air Ace

UP, UP, AND AWAY
THE HISTORY OF AVIATION

© B4U Publishing for Albatros,
an imprint of Albatros Media Group, 2025
5. května 1746/22, Prague 4, Czech Republic
Author: Tomáš SMOT Svoboda
Illustrator: © Tomáš SMOT Svoboda, 2024
Editors: Štěpánka Sekaninová, Tom Velčovský
Translator: Andrew Oakland
Proofreader: Scott Alexander Jones

Graphics and typesetting: Martin Urbánek
& Tomáš SMOT Svoboda

Printed in China by Leo Paper Group Ltd.

www.albatrosbooks.com

 albatros

BOOKS I REALLY ENJOYED, AND YOU WILL TOO.

The Aircraft Book: The Definitive Visual History, by DK, 2021

Means of Transport That Changed the World,
by Štěpánka Sekaninová, Tom Velčovský; Albatros, 2022

Means of Transport That Almost Changed the World,
by Štěpánka Sekaninová, Tom Velčovský; Albatros, 2023

*The Encyclopedia of Modern Aircraft: From Civilian Airliners
to Military Superfighters*, by Jim Winchester; Thunder Bay Press, 2006

WHICH IS FASTEST?

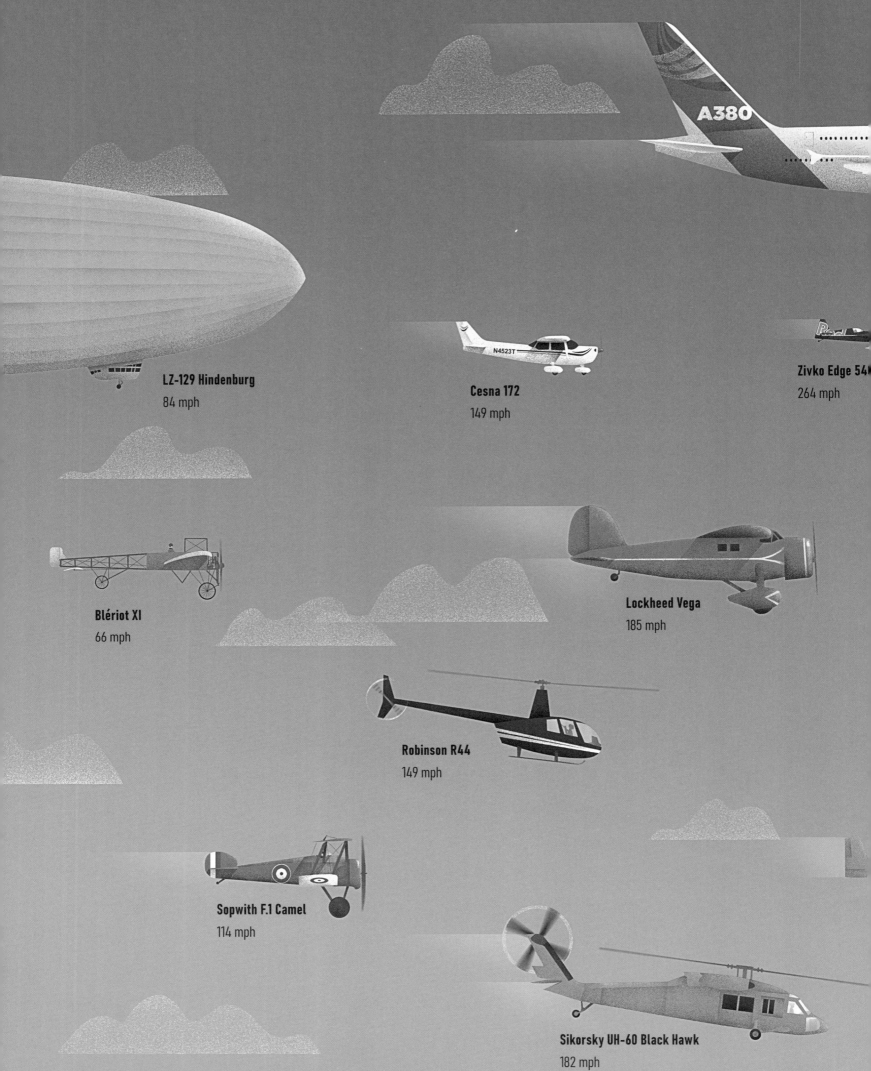

A380

LZ-129 Hindenburg
84 mph

Cesna 172
149 mph

Zivko Edge 54
264 mph

Blériot XI
66 mph

Lockheed Vega
185 mph

Robinson R44
149 mph

Sopwith F.1 Camel
114 mph

Sikorsky UH-60 Black Hawk
182 mph